Television
and the
Teaching of
English

Television and the Teaching of English

BY **NEIL POSTMAN**

AND THE COMMITTEE ON THE STUDY OF TELEVISION
OF THE NATIONAL COUNCIL OF TEACHERS OF ENGLISH

APPLETON-CENTURY-CROFTS, INC.
NEW YORK

PRINTED IN THE UNITED STATES OF AMERICA

Foreword

This book grew from the co-operative efforts of many people.

For some time, the members of the Committee on the Study of Television of the National Council of Teachers of English had wanted to prepare a book on television that would suggest ways in which the relatively untapped strength of this youngest of the communications media could be identified and utilized in the teaching of English, literature, and language arts. The distance between dream and reality, however, was great until we were given substantial encouragement and assistance by Louis Hausman, Director of the Television Information Office, who recognized the potential significance of the project. Through his support we were given access to technical information, sources of material, discussions with creative television people, and helpful criticism.

We are indebted to several people who shared their ideas with Dr. Postman. Among these are Robert Herridge, producer-director of *The Robert Herridge Theater;* Don Richardson, director of *The World of Sholem Aleichem* and *Lullaby;* Gore Vidal, author of *A Visit to a Small Planet* and other television plays; Peter Cott of the Academy of Television Arts and Sciences; Lawrence Creshkoff of the Television Information Office; Dennis Knife of the television program *Candid Camera;* Judith Greene, formerly of the television series, *Project 20;* George Gordon of New York University; Howard Damon of New York University; Max Bogart of the New Jersey State Education Department; and, Paul Kozelka of Teachers College, Columbia University.

Special thanks are due to Dean Lester Asheim of the Graduate Library School of the University of Chicago, whose doctoral dissertation, *From Book to Film: A Comparative Analysis of the Content of Novels and the Motion Pictures Based Upon Them,* suggested the categories and some of the questions of the "cross-media" procedures which appear on pages 92-95. Milton Kaplan, a member of the Committee on the Study of Television of the National Council of Teachers of English, graciously allowed parts of an unpublished article to be incorporated into Part Two of the book. In fact, the manner in which Part Two is organized merely duplicates the pattern originally devised by Dr. Kaplan.

This book was read and approved by the Committee on Publications of the National Council of Teachers of English, consisting of Muriel Crosby of the Wilmington, Delaware Public Schools, William S. Ward of the University of Kentucky, Robert Bennett of the Minneapolis Public Schools and James R. Squire, Executive Secretary of the National Council of Teachers of English and Chairman of the Committee. Other readers who gave helpful suggestions were William Hoth of Wayne State University, Fred Marcus of Los Angeles State College, and Enid Olson, Publications Associate of the National Council of Teachers of English.

Members of the Committee on the Study of Television who conceived of the project and who worked closely at every point in the venture, giving constant guidance and support to Dr. Postman, are listed below:

Martha Gable
   Director of Television
   Philadelphia Public Schools

Patrick Hazard
   Annenberg School of Communication
   University of Pennsylvania
   Philadelphia, Pennsylvania

Henry Maloney
   Cooley High School
   Detroit, Michigan

Alice Sterner
   Barringer High School
   Newark, New Jersey

Morris Goldberger
Scholastic Book Services
   New York, New York

Milton Kaplan
   George Washington High School
   New York, New York

Joseph Mersand
   Jamaica High School
   New York, New York

Finally, the Committee on the Study of Television wants to express its gratitude to Neil Postman who worked in such good humor with eight "bosses"—members of the Committee —who developed the general plan of the book and who criticized its several drafts.

Louis Forsdale
Chairman, NCTE Committee on the Study of Television

Teachers College
Columbia University

Contents

Foreword   v

Introduction   1

PART ONE: *The Educational Significance
of Television*   3

CHAPTER

1. Mass Communication: A Review and a Perspective   5

2. Television: The Invention and The Industry   14

3. Television and Its Effects   30

4. The Literature of Television   39

PART TWO: *The Classroom Study of Television*   75

PROCEDURE

1. Announcement on Bulletin Board   77

2. Announcement Made in Class   78

3. Display on Bulletin Board   79

4. Student Television Committee   80

5. Special Class Assignment   82

6. Brief Unit Isolated From Regular Curriculum   88

7. Brief Unit Within the Regular Curriculum   92

8. Extensive Unit   105

9. Course in Television   115

10. Workshop in Television   129

Glossary   131

Bibliography   135

Television
and the
Teaching of
English

Introduction

By giving it an unprecedented opportunity to function in new contexts and to appear in new forms, television has extended the force and influence of the English language. What becomes of this opportunity will depend in large measure on the millions of youngsters for whom television is the most persistent and magnetic source of information and a primary source of literary experience. To the extent that their responses to television are informed, discriminating, and creative, we may be assured that our language and literature, as well as the lives of our students, will be enriched by contact with television. But taste and critical judgment are learned habits of mind. As a consequence, education, as in most things, is the decisive factor.

The ultimate purpose of this book is to contribute toward the "television education" of our students. The immediate goal of the book is to offer motivation, aid, and confidence to teachers of English who wish to help their students obtain that education.

Teachers of English are singled out because it is they who have the major responsibility for teaching students how to develop those skills that will enable them to respond with satisfaction and intelligence to diverse communication forms. The English teacher, more than any other, is concerned with those media through which our language and literature are given form. The newspaper, the magazine, the film, the radio —each of these media has challenged the resourcefulness and virtuosity of the English teacher. Television presents still another challenge.

This book is divided into two parts. Part One provides teachers with a perspective, and some of the information and vocabulary they will need in order to think and teach about television as an educational and cultural medium. No attempt has been made to deal with *all* of television. The word *television* is a high-level abstraction which refers to many and various kinds of activities. For this reason, the book discusses only those aspects of television in which the English teacher would have some special interest or which are essential to an understanding of the medium. These would include, for example, some consideration of television's place in communication history, its artistic resources, its economic structure, its social effects, its literary forms. Wherever possible, these discussions reflect interviews with people who are professionally concerned with television.

Part Two of the book suggests to teachers specific methods, materials, and activities for teaching about television. The suggestions and procedures in Part Two give consideration to the great differences in the backgrounds of teachers, the kinds of students whom they instruct, and the varieties of English curricula within which they must function. Not every teacher will use all of these suggestions. However, any interested teacher can find something of value in this section.

NEIL POSTMAN
Associate Professor of
English Education
New York University

PART ONE

The
Educational
Significance
of
Television

CHAPTER ONE

Mass Communication: A Review and a Perspective

In any elementary or high school classroom in the United States, the teacher is probably the only member of the group who can recall vividly a time when life was lived without television. But the children are likely to be unaware of this "phenomenon." They take their television for granted. Young teachers, for their part, may take the radio for granted since they probably do not remember life without radio. Memory is thus wholly inadequate for providing us with that sense of perspective which allows us to see our present condition as part of an unending process of change, accommodation to change, and further change.

A historical perspective of modes of mass communication is needed. Perhaps such a perspective will demonstrate that we have entered a period in history in which we have access, as writers, readers, listeners, and viewers, to the widest range of expressiveness that man has ever known. This sense of media history may well encourage the teacher to welcome television as a most compelling addition to this spectrum and deepen his concern for the full realization of its potentialities.

SPEECH

No one has ever found a human community that did not possess a language fully developed for the purposes of its users, if by *language* we mean speech or a structured system of vocal symbols. Speech was probably not only the first instrument of mass communication, but, even more important, was also the means by which man decisively and qualitatively differentiated himself from all other forms of life. More than the tool-making animal, man is the symbolizing animal. He alone can transform sound into the subtlest expressions of mind, and by definition there is no human tradition older than the oral tradition.

Practically nothing is known about the origins of language except that men adapted organs of breathing and eating to the purpose of talking and have probably been making meaningful sounds at each other for at least 100,000 years. Although speech continues to be the most widely used symbolic device among men, as well as their basic mechanism of social integration, it is difficult for any of us to imagine a world in which speech serves as the only practice of language. For Western civilization, that world ended with the invention of the alphabet.

WRITING

Our alphabet was invented by the Syrio-Palestinian Semites about 1500 B.C. and was carried to completion by the Phoenicians. Whereas speech is a primary or direct symbolization of events, processes, and things in the world, alphabetic writing is a set of symbols of a set of symbols; that is, an attempt to represent the sounds of human speech by a system of graphic signs. Through writing, the continuous flow of sounds that is speech was captured, as by a camera, and made motionless. In so doing man extended his language beyond the "natural" limitations of time and space. At first, man struggled with his new invention, affixing signs to almost any surface that could retain them with some degree of permanence. He tried, at one time or another, bark, wax, clay, leather, papyrus, and vellum, on which surfaces he scratched, chiseled, or hammered. By the middle of the fourth century B.C., the Ionic alphabet of twenty-four letters had become standardized, and the portable and unpretentious papyrus scrolls of the Greeks were the best instrument for recording and preserving human speech that had yet emerged. Nevertheless, this transmutation of language did not meet with uniform approval. One of the facts that invariably emerges from any study of human communication is that anxiety, suspicion, and pessimism accompany communication changes. Men tend to resent the intrusion of a new medium of communication and often feel compelled to defend the older medium against anticipated or actual competition. Socrates, for example, wrote no books and believed that they were inferior to the spoken word as a means of education. In Plato's *Phaedrus* several significant passages express Socrates' hostility to the written word. The following is among the most familiar:

> A terrible thing about writing, Phaedrus, is this, and here, in truth, it is like painting. I mean, the creations of the painter stand like living creatures, but if you ask them anything, they maintain a solemn silence. And so it is with writings; you might think they spoke as if they had intelligence, but if you put a question with a wish for information on a point in what is said, there is one, one only, invariable reply. Further, once a word is written, it goes rolling all about, comes indifferently among those who understand it and those whom it no wise concerns, and is unaware to whom it should address itself and to whom it should not do so.

But private prejudice is not a persevering antagonist to the movement of history. The invention of writing produced a chain of more or less radical reactions at almost every level of society. Writing, for instance, favored the progress of commerce; and light writing materials, in particular, led to the expansion of city-states into empires. Writing also tended to fix historical tradition and strengthen social cohesion. It encouraged an interest in science, contributed toward the development of Roman law, and facilitated the spread of Christianity.

On the other hand, throughout the entire period of "unmechanized" writing—from the clay tablet to the handwritten book—the spoken word remained pre-eminent. It was the main instrument of instruction, political persuasion, and literary experience. Homer's poetry was invariably recited. Herodotus publicly read his histories. One school of philosophy —Stoicism—was named after the porches from which its advocates talked. Cicero, the greatest of Roman orators, composed his speeches by saying them, and only later did he write them down. In fact, all classical literature—poetry, drama, philosophy, history—was intended to be heard rather than read. Even well into the medieval period, language was essentially a medium of the ear, and almost all organized learning, both in and out of the school, was received by auditory methods. Students came to class, sat at the feet of their instructors, and listened. For all practical purposes, they had no sources of information or ideas other than the spoken words of their teachers. Written assignments and written examinations were unknown. There was no such thing as a slate or a blackboard. When students read from manuscripts, their pace was apparently extremely slow, even tortuous, as they "spelled" their way through each sheet somewhat in the manner of the uneducated reader of today. In short, the spoken word was the main channel of communication even in the face of competition from the handwritten manuscript. Not until the invention of print did another linguistic medium drastically intrude on man's symbolic consciousness.

PRINT

The exact year and place in which the printing press of Western civilization was invented is somewhat in doubt. Seven cities, in fact, have claimed the honor, each fixing the date at a time different from the others. But it is generally accepted that Johann Gensfleisch zum Gutenberg, a goldsmith from the city of Mainz in Germany, produced the first "artificial script" in the year 1456. This was the famous and still extant forty-two-line Bible. Before the century was over, in almost every country in Europe, books were being printed, as Gutenberg put it, "without the help of reed, stylus, or pen but by the wondrous agreement, proportion, and harmony of punches and types."

Printing was, from its beginning, a successful commercial venture. The new medium had no such formidable adversary as Socrates. Resistance to it came largely from those who had collected expensive libraries of manuscripts or those whose livelihood depended on manuscripts, namely, writers of text-hand. For the latter, the printing press was, so to speak, the handwriting on the wall.

Print, in even more revolutionary ways than writing, changed the very form of civilization. It is not entirely coincidence, for instance, that the Protestant Reformation was contemporaneous with the invention of movable type. From the time Martin Luther posted his theses in 1517, the printing press was used to publish controversial, even inflammatory, religious tracts. But even more important, the printing and distribution of millions of Bibles made possible a more personal religion, as the Word of God rested on each man's kitchen table.

The book, by isolating the reader and his responses, tended to separate him from the powerful oral influences of his family, teacher, and priest. Print thus created a new conception of self as well as of self-interest. At the same time, the printing press provided the wide circulation necessary to create national literatures and intense pride in one's native language. Print thus promoted individualism on the one hand and nationalism on the other.

Printing also created new literary forms and altered ideas of literary style. Medieval poetry was conceived for the ear, and each poem had to stand the test of recitation. In addition, medieval audiences were not always interested in the poet himself, since his work was known to them only through the interpretations of minstrels who frequently rephrased poems to suit their own image and images. The printed page changed these conditions. Slowly, the printed poet came into a new relationship with his reader. He learned not to be as repetitive as his predecessors since a reader could be depended upon to return as often as needed to uncomprehended passages. He learned also to create rhymes and syntax for the eye as well as the ear, as John Donne did in his sermons. The form of the printed page itself provided a visual means of differentiating poetry from prose and added new dimensions to the art of versification. Prose assumed new forms, such as the personal essays of Montaigne and the novels of Defoe and Richardson, the last of whom was himself a printer. After the flowering of dramatic poetry during the Elizabethan Age, the printed page substituted for the theater, and millions of school children came to know Shakespeare only through this form.

In schools, print shifted the emphasis from oral to written and visual communication. Teachers who had been only partly concerned with instructing their students in how to read became by mid-sixteenth century concerned with almost nothing else. Since the sixteenth century, the textbook has been a primary source of income for book publishers. Since the sixteenth century, written examinations and written assignments have been an integral part of the methodology of school teaching; and since the sixteenth century, the image of the isolated student, the student who reads and studies by himself, has been the essence of our conception of scholarship. In short, for 400 years Western civilization has lived in what has been characterized as the "Age of Gutenberg." Print has been the chief means of our information flow. Print has shaped our literature and conditioned our responses to literary experience. Print has influenced our conception of the educational process.

THE COMMUNICATIONS REVOLUTION

Certainly printed media and the printed book in particular will continue to exert powerful influences on our society. Once they have become literate, most people have intellectual and emotional powers that are irrevocable. But equally certain is the fact that print no longer "monopolizes man's symbolic environment," to use David Riesman's phrase. That monopoly began to dissolve toward the middle of the nineteenth century, when a more or less continuous stream of media inventions began to make accessible unprecedented quantities of information and created new modes of perception and qualities of aesthetic experience. To select a specific year as marking the beginning of the "technological revolution" is difficult; but 1839 is chosen because, in that year, Daguerre developed the first practical method of photography. In 1844, Morse perfected the telegraph. In 1876, Bell transmitted the first telephone message. A year later, Edison invented the phonograph. By 1894, the movies had also been introduced. A year after that, Marconi sent and received the first wireless message. In 1906, Fessenden transmitted the human voice by radio. In 1920, regularly scheduled radio broadcasts began. In 1923, a picture was televised between New York and Philadelphia. In that same year, Henry Luce and Briton Hadden created a totally new idea in magazines with *Time*. In 1927, the first "talkie" appeared; and in 1928, Disney's first animated cartoon. In 1935, Major E. H. Armstrong developed the FM radio. In 1936 came *Life* magazine. In 1941, full commercial television was authorized. These are just some of the inventions that form a part of the "communications revolution" through which we are all living. To these could be added, of course, the LP record, the tape recorder, the comic strip, the comic book, the tabloid newspaper, the electronic computer, the paperback book.

I feel this—and I feel it passionately—people who deny themselves television deny themselves participation in life today. They are horse-and-buggy; they are atrophied; they are self-exiled from the world. They suffer from the most painful illiteracy, which is that of the literate.

In terms of reporting conversation, ideas or drama, television can do something that no other medium has done. And for the viewer, the responsibility of self-editing, of selection, is the same as in choosing a book, a play or a motion picture. It becomes an exercise of will; a demonstration of taste.

John Mason Brown
From an interview with J. P. Shanley as reported in *The New York Times*, July 21, 1957.

What this burgeoning of mass media means and will mean to our society is difficult to assess. Perhaps we are at a point where we can only ask questions. Many come to mind. For instance, if the telegraph made nothing so old as yesterday's newspaper, have radio and television similarly made some of the functions of *today's* newspaper obsolescent? If photography changed the character of painting, has the film challenged the novel to invent new means of expression? Now that the flow of information in our culture is so continuous and its sources so various, do we run the risk of being overwhelmed by facts? (One thinks of the little girl whose one-line book report read: "This book told me more about penguins than I wanted to know.")

The quality of our responses to these and other questions will depend largely on how much we know about each of the new media. Many teachers have felt that because of the multiplication of the sources of symbolic experience a redefinition of "literacy" is required, one that would extend beyond the printed page. These teachers assume that there is no useful cause to be served by intensifying or exaggerating whatever conflicts may seem to exist between media, such as television and the printed word. While a new medium of communication invariably engages in serious competition with older media for prestige and attention, surely the printed word has continued to thrive in the midst of an electronic revolution. Since 1939, Americans have purchased more than two billion paperback books alone. Teachers, quite obviously, must continue to teach the arts of the printed word, as they have done for centuries.

On the other hand, teachers probably need to accustom themselves to the serious possibility that print, their preferred or "natural" medium, is not necessarily the preferred medium of the youngsters whom they teach. As Malcolm Cowley says in the essay, "The Next Fifty Years in American Literature":

> A final possibility must be considered that printed literature in the future will be written for and read only by scholars. For the public at large it might give way to picture books, or to spoken and tape-recorded stories, or else to dramas and serials composed for television or the new medium that will come after it.
>
> Whatever the new forms may be, I am not at all sure that I shall like them when they do appear. They won't be my forms and won't express my spirit, but I know they are needed if the new age is to become fully conscious of its own spirit.

Whatever the future may hold, teachers of English can face it with equanimity if they avoid the temptation to pit television or any other medium against print. A more realistic and challenging point of view is to regard the coexistence of these forms as a more or less permanent arrangement and aim at making students "literate" in the various media which engage their attention. Any other policy would be unbecoming to a great profession.

CHAPTER TWO

Television:

The Invention and
the Industry

In the preceding chapter, speech, writing, print, and the newer media were referred to as "mass media" because each is capable of transmitting symbolic messages to large numbers of people. But the term *mass media* requires further definition if we are to understand the various contexts in which it may be used and especially if we are to understand the nature of television.

In particular, a distinction needs to be drawn between the instruments or media of communication and the uses to which they are put. Communication, defined in its basic and most human terms, is a process of exchanging symbolic meaning. The media which serve this process are many and varied: sound as in the spoken language, graphics and paper as in the written word, stone as in the carved image, photographic images projected in rapid succession as in the movies. Any particular medium may or may not be a "mass medium" depending entirely on its use. There are millions of people in this country who create and then become, along with their helpless relatives, the audience for "home" movies. In this context and form, the film cannot be designated as a mass medium. Nor can television be so designated when it is used in "closed-circuit," or radio when it is in the hands of a "ham operator." However, it is obvious that the use of a particular

14

medium is dictated to a large extent by characteristics intrinsic to the medium. For instance, the cost of producing a 35 mm. film—even without professional actors, as in the case of Robert Flaherty's documentaries—is so high that it is impossible to make such a film for the exclusive enjoyment of oneself and one's relatives. The cost of broadcasting through the air is similarly prohibitive.

We may say, then, that certain media, by their very structure, enforce their use as "mass media." Typically, television, radio, movies, newspapers, and magazines are so used and so regarded. They are mass media in a different sense from, say, the English language, the Cathedral at Chartres, or Beethoven's *Ninth Symphony,* each of which communicates meaning to large numbers of people. The mass media such as radio and television are products of a technological culture and have in common not only their large and heterogeneous audiences but also their high cost of operation and multiple divisions of creative and technical labor. In addition, these "mechanized" media transmit messages that are, to a more or less degree, received simultaneously by an audience. Although the term *mass audience* tends to be misleading since it connotes identical responses from all listeners, the members of an audience of a mass medium certainly have limited means for communicating with each other, which is to say that they tend to be an anonymous audience. In view of these factors, much interest has developed concerning the legal and economic aspects of the mass media. The virtual omnipresence of the media, their key role in the economy, the size and anonymity of their audiences, the simultaneous reception of their messages, all of these intimate a degree of potential influence that might engender in some people a sense of uneasiness if they do not understand the total context in which the media operate.

For this reason a consideration of television might well begin with discussions of the economic, institutional, and legal forces which merge to form its nature.

THE INVENTION

The process of invention invariably involves a reshuffling and recombination of already existing facts and materials. But insofar as the word *invention* connotes a single conceptual leap by the imagination of one man, television was not "invented" at all. It evolved, step by step, with many men at various times contributing to its ultimate form. Television, for example, is essentially a process involving the transmission of electromagnetic energy; thus, names usually associated with other inventions and media—Faraday, Morse, Marconi, DeForest, to name a few—are also linked with the invention of television.

If, however, a specific year must be chosen to mark the beginning of television in America, it most likely would be 1923, when Vladimir Zworykin, a research scientist then at Westinghouse and later at RCA, applied for a patent on the iconoscope, an electronic scanning device and picture tube. Subsequent refinements were developed by such research laboratories and individual inventors as American Telephone and Telegraph, General Electric, the Radio Corporation of America, Allen B. Dumont, and Philo Farnsworth. The most recent major refinement was color television. More than 360 stations are equipped to rebroadcast network color programs. Trade publications estimate that there are now more than a half million color television sets in America.

THE FEDERAL COMMUNICATIONS COMMISSION

The history of legislation dealing with radio in the United States began in 1910, when most radio transmission still consisted of what was then called "wireless telegraphy"—the sending of signals in the famous dot-and-dash Morse Code.

Under a Congressional amendment to the Interstate Commerce Act in that year, wireless as well as wire communication (telegraph and telephone) came under federal jurisdiction.

Also in 1910, the Wireless Ship Act established certain requirements for the installation of radio equipment on passenger vessels. More specific regulation did not seem called for until technical advances made possible the transmission of speech and music—instead of dots and dashes—and sparked a growing interest in radio. Now it became possible for relatively untrained personnel to send messages. In addition to ships and commercial communication companies, government agencies, high school and college physics classes, and hobbyists at home began building their own radio receivers and even transmitters.

Soon the air began to be filled with conflicting signals. In 1912, partly as a result of the *Titanic* disaster, when radio communication with the mainland was partially obstructed by interfering signals, the first Radio Act was passed. This legislation empowered the Secretary of Commerce to grant a license to any United States citizen who wished to operate a transmitter. Many of the applicants were manufacturers of radio receivers who wanted to provide a program service for people who bought their equipment. With the government's discretionary powers restricted to the assignment of a limited number of frequencies, and with more and more applicants asking for licenses, the channels assigned to broadcasting became increasingly crowded.

Between 1922 and 1925, many responsible broadcasters meeting in annual conference at the invitation of Secretary of Commerce Herbert Hoover made recommendations for laying down ground rules for the broadcasting industry. Basic to these recommendations was a recognition that the "space" limitations imposed by the nature of the radio spectrum required a certain measure of government control. Someone had to have enforceable power to make frequency assignments and to insist upon maintenance of certain standards in the operation of broadcast stations.

The Radio Act of 1927 (and its extension, the Communications Act of 1934) incorporated many of the recommendations that came out of the Fourth Radio Conference (1925), and ultimately established an independent regulatory commission to represent the Congress in assuring adherence to the provisions of the law. In addition to establishing the power of the government to regulate broadcasting by assigning frequencies, the fundamental communications laws also articulated the basic principles that the radio spectrum is a national resource in which all the people retain an interest, and that frequencies may be used for private purposes only if such purposes are in the public interest.

From 1927 to 1934, regulation of broadcasting was under the five-member Federal Radio Commission. Since 1934, the regulatory agency for radio and television broadcasting has been the seven-member Federal Communications Commission, whose members are appointed by the President, generally for staggered terms of seven years. One of the most important powers of the Commission is the granting of broadcasting licenses to those applicants whom it deems worthy of public trust. To help the FCC make this determination, an applicant is required to provide the Commission with, among other things, information about his financial responsibility, technical competence, and proposed programming schedule. Licenses are generally issued for a three-year period, and may be revoked or not renewed if the licensee does not conform to the requirements of his mandate to serve the "public interest, convenience, and necessity."

One of the most difficult problems confronting the FCC is how to accommodate a continuing demand for television licenses in the face of the limited number of channels allocated to television broadcasting. When television began its phenomenal growth after World War II, only 12 channels were available. These channels, numbered from 2 to 13, are all in the Very High Frequency (VHF) portion of the electromagnetic spectrum. (By contrast, 107 channels are allocated to standard radio broadcasting, and 100 channels to FM.) In 1952, after

108 VHF stations had begun broadcasting and more than 15 million families had purchased VHF receivers, the FCC added 70 television channels in a new and relatively unexplored part of the spectrum known as Ultra High Frequency (UHF). By utilizing 82 channels, the 1952 allocations plan visualized as many as 2,100 stations in some 1,300 communities throughout the country. However, television broadcasting is still largely confined to the 12 VHF channels; of 527 commercial stations operating at the beginning of 1961 only 76 were in the UHF band.

Sec. 315. (a) If any licensee shall permit any person who is a legally qualified candidate for any public office to use a broadcasting station, he shall afford equal opportunities to all other such candidates for that office in the use of such broadcasting station: Provided, That such licensee shall have no power of censorship over the material broadcast under the provisions of this section. No obligation is hereby imposed upon any licensee to allow the use of its station by any such candidate. Appearance by a legally qualified candidate on any—

(1) bona fide newscast,

(2) bona fide news interview,

(3) bona fide news documentary (if the appearance of the candidate is incidental to the presentation of the subject or subjects covered by the news documentary), or

(4) on-the-spot coverage of bona fide news events (including but not limited to political conventions and activities incidental thereto), shall not be deemed to be use of a broadcasting station within the meaning of this subsection. Nothing in the foregoing sentence shall be construed as relieving broadcasters, in connection with the presentation of newscasts, news interviews, news documentaries, and on-the-spot coverage of news events, from the obligation imposed upon them under this Act to operate in the public interest and to afford

> reasonable opportunity for the discussion of conflicting views on issues of public importance.
>
> * * * *
>
> Sec. 326. Nothing in this Act shall be understood or construed to give the Commission the power of censorship over the radio communications or signals transmitted by any radio station, and no regulation or condition shall be promulgated or fixed by the Commission which shall interfere with the right of free speech by means of radio communication.
>
> *Communications Act of 1934, as Amended*

Although in some flat, open areas UHF transmitters provide service quite comparable to that provided by similarly located VHF transmitters, the propagation of television signals over hilly or mountainous terrain has proved to be less satisfactory in the UHF than in the VHF band, and, as a rule, UHF signals have not covered as wide an area. While UHF television has been found to be substantially freer from atmospheric interference and such man-made interferences as ignition noise and airplane flutter, it has been more subject to obstruction from trees and tall buildings. In many areas served by both VHF and UHF stations, television set owners who bought their receivers before the introduction of UHF have been reluctant to go to the expense of making the installation necessary to receive UHF signals, and equipment manufacturers have not succeeded in producing all-channel receivers that could be sold at the same price as VHF-only receivers.

Given this combination of circumstances, many UHF stations have been unable to become economically viable, especially where they have been in direct competition with VHF stations. By the end of 1960, 99 of the 185 UHF stations that had been built and operated were no longer on the air; 243 of the 380 construction permits issued by the FCC for UHF stations since 1952 have been voluntarily surrendered.

The FCC has before it a number of proposals to deal with the problem of UHF versus VHF. These include recommending legislation that would permit only all-channel receivers to be shipped in interstate commerce, changing channel assignments so that all communities would be either VHF or UHF but not both, and eliminating VHF entirely in favor of an all-UHF system. But all the proposed solutions raise great problems of service and economics for both broadcasters and the viewing public.

Another major problem which the FCC has had to face grows out of the vague legal language used to describe the public responsibilities of broadcasters. The Communications Act prohibits transmission of profane and obscene language, and requires that competing, bona fide candidates for office be provided with equal time and facilities for political broadcasts. Additionally, the Act requires the broadcaster to treat controversial issues in a manner that will ensure fairness to differing points of view. It also directly forbids the Commission from passing judgment on a program before it is broadcast and from interfering with the right of free speech. But the Act does not go beyond these proscriptions with any degree of specificity. Although the courts have consistently upheld the Commission's right to pass judgment on the program performance of a station, or, to use Justice Frankfurter's phrase, to decide "the composition of the traffic," the FCC has not meticulously defined for itself, for the public, or for the industry what precisely constitutes broadcasting in the public interest. The establishment of a workable definition is, and probably will continue to be, one of the thorniest problems faced by the Commission and the broadcaster. Nevertheless, the FCC exists as both a symbol of the broadcaster's responsibility to the public and a legal agency through which that responsibility may be enforced.

THE SPONSOR

Except for noncommercial educational TV stations, revenue from advertising pays all the costs of television broadcasting in the United States—non-sponsored programs as well as sponsored. In contrast to pay TV, "free" television does not require its audiences to pay money directly to broadcasters. Nor, as in the case of some foreign systems, does the set owner pay an annual license fee. The audience does, of course, invest money in the purchase and maintenance of its receivers, and pays for the electric power necessary to operate them. Also, the audience buys the products advertised on television, thereby indirectly contributing to the advertising budget. Thus, advertising may properly be regarded as the economic base on which television broadcasting rests.

Advertising on television has proved to be extremely effective. For many corporations, in fact, television is the primary advertising medium. Of some 1.7 billion dollars spent during 1959 for time and space in television, radio, newspapers, magazines, and outdoor advertising by the 100 largest national advertisers, 51 per cent was invested in television.

Over the years, three distinct ways have developed for buying advertising time on television. On both the networks and local stations, the advertiser can buy a complete program or participation within a program; on local stations, he can also buy a "spot announcement" (a brief time period that is adjacent to a program).

When an advertiser buys a program, he becomes its sponsor, and tends to be identified with the program in the public mind. He is, of course, interested in pleasing the public, and his program choice depends on what kind of audience he is trying to reach. Frequently the sponsor wants primarily to attract the largest possible audience, in which case he will buy programs that have demonstrated their capacity to do this. Certain advertisers are interested in reaching a more specialized audience, one that may be somewhat smaller but is likely to be attracted to programming like symphonic music, serious drama, or documentaries. Specific details vary from situation to situation but the advertiser who sponsors a program undertakes to pay the costs—which are frequently considerable—of producing the program as well as buying the time period on the station or network on which it is to be shown. In recent years, advertisers often have bought programs on a shared sponsorship basis, as alternate sponsors or co-sponsors.

Certain programs permit advertising participation by a number of different advertisers. In these cases, the program and time costs for the entire program are prorated and shared by all the participating advertisers, with predetermined time periods set aside for the commercial messages. Such programs are usually owned by the network or station. The advertiser merely is afforded the opportunity to present his commercial message in an environment which he considers compatible with his product or message.

Still another form of advertising on television is the "spot" commercial, which is broadcast between programs or at intervals within programs. Periods of ten, twenty or sixty seconds duration are made available for advertising that is not necessarily related to the program within which it appears or to which it is adjacent. The sale of time for "spot" commercials represents one of the principal sources of income for local stations.

The decisions that a television advertiser makes as to what form or combination of forms of advertising he will buy are dependent on what is available, and on his judgment as to what will be best for his company's welfare. Thus, commercial television, like other forms of mass communication, is shaped to a considerable extent by the needs of the business community. From the standpoint of the public welfare, there are both advantages and disadvantages to advertiser-supported television.

The most obvious advantage is that the advertiser, not the audience, pays for the high costs of producing and broadcasting television programs. Another advantage, although a negative one, is that the alternatives to our present commercial system might present greater problems than those they claim to solve. For example, government-operated networks might involve the risk of their developing into either "Republican" or "Democratic" television. They might also be vulnerable to organized pressure groups with inordinate political influence. Also, not only does the advertiser provide useful commercial information to the public, but under our economic system the marketing and distribution of goods and services is generally recognized as a primary element in the maintenance of a high standard of living. Television advertising has demonstrated its effectiveness as a marketing tool.

On the other hand, several objections are raised about advertiser-supported television. In the first place, some critics object that the sponsor, motivated by purely commercial considerations, presents only programs that are of interest to the largest possible audience. Thus, he fails to support programs that are of special interest to "cultural minorities." In the second place, the sponsor will sometimes delete from his program material that may be considered controversial, unpopular, or even stimulating, since there are occasions when a sponsor does not desire to stimulate audiences beyond the point at which they are simply good consumers. In the third place, during the course of a sponsored program, some advertisers, invoking the right to sell their wares, will interrupt the broadcast for that purpose with minimal regard to the artistic integrity of the presentation. Such intrusions tend to dissipate the artistic power of the medium.

By contrast, there are notable instances of sponsors—Alcoa, Armstrong, Bell & Howell, Esso, Hallmark, Olin Mathieson, Purex, to name a few—which have consistently given producers, writers, and directors the greatest possible freedom of performance, and have provided programs of artistic and political importance. In addition, there are certain types of programs which by station or network policy are not exposed to sponsor influence, specifically news and public affairs programs.

Nevertheless, some of the problems inherent in the sponsored system of broadcasting have not yet been entirely solved and continue to engage the attention of the many responsible people in the industry.

THE NETWORKS

There are three nationwide television networks: American Broadcasting Company (ABC); Columbia Broadcasting System (CBS); and National Broadcasting Company (NBC). By connecting program origination points with a large number of television stations, networks make possible the instantaneous broadcasting of programs throughout the country. This has the effect of amortizing the cost of expensive programs over a large number of viewers. The cost of producing the *Ed Sullivan Show,* or *Hallmark Hall of Fame,* or *Winston Churchill: The Valiant Years* would be substantially the same whether it were broadcast by a single station or by a network. (Few, if any, stations could afford to produce such programs just for their own use.) By providing a simultaneous nationwide audience, the networks can make sponsorship of such programs attractive to advertisers. Furthermore, through the maintenance of highly trained news and public affairs staffs throughout the world, networks are able to inform the public quickly and effectively on problems of vital interest. Whether such programs are sponsored or—as in the case of the television "debates" between the presidential candidates in 1960—not sponsored, the existence of the networks makes such news and informational services possible.

Thus, the primary function of a network is as a supplier

and distributor of a program service. But, the network companies are also station owners; each owns five VHF stations, the maximum permitted by law. Since network programs are private communications until they are broadcast from a station's transmitter, the networks as networks are not required to be licensed by the Federal Communications Commission. Only through the licensed stations owned by network companies is some degree of indirect regulation over the networks exercised by the FCC.

THE LOCAL STATION

Of the nearly 600 commercial television stations operating in the United States, all but twenty are affiliated with at least one of the networks. The great majority of the unaffiliated stations are in major metropolitan areas like New York, Chicago, Los Angeles, St. Louis, Washington, D. C., San Francisco. But in most communities, the individual stations have entered into affiliation agreements with individual networks whereby they broadcast the programs of that network to the viewers in their area.

Through its network affiliation, a local station has a regular source of programming and shares in the revenue derived by the network from the sale of the network programs broadcast over that station. However, an even more important source of income for a local station is the sale of time for "spot" commercials in station-break periods adjacent to network programs. Because of the ability of many network programs to draw large audiences, these station-break positions are particularly attractive to advertisers.

The local broadcaster also has other sources of programming. He buys syndicated programs on film and tape from independent producers (much as local newspapers buy syndicated columns by such people as Walter Lippmann and Walter Winchell), and he buys feature films from film distributors. An important aspect of local station operation is the production of local live programs, particularly in areas of news, public affairs, information, and education. Many such programs are produced in collaboration with schools, colleges, universities, museums, and other educational institutions.

Because a high proportion of programs that are seen and heard daily at "prime" times are originated by them, the networks have considerable influence and prestige. This fact invests them with a great deal of responsibility for the quality of broadcasting in America. It should be stressed, though, that the owner of an individual station, affiliated or not, is responsible under the Communications Act for the operation of his station.

EDUCATIONAL TELEVISION

In addition to the commercial operation, an alternative system of television service is available to many Americans (approximately forty million of them). This "second service" is supplied by the Educational Television (ETV) stations.

From the standpoint of its methods of transmission, noncommercial ETV operates in the same manner as commercial television. The two differ in terms of purpose and financing. The ETV stations operate on channels reserved by the Federal Communications Commission in 1952 explicitly for noncommercial educational use. Specifically, 258 channels have been set aside for this purpose. Although only about sixty are currently in operation, their number is steadily increasing. The costs of operating ETV stations throughout the United States are met partly by money from public tax funds and partly by money from foundations and private contributors. By law, noncommercial ETV stations may not sell broadcasting time to sponsors.

Typically, ETV stations provide programs that are of interest to special groups within a community, which is to say that such programs may not be "popular" enough to attract great audiences. Although all ETV stations offer some programs of a general "cultural and entertainment" nature, ETV programming is characterized by specialized, technical, and instructional presentations. Indeed, the theory of a "second service" such as ETV provides rests on the assumption that commercial broadcasting cannot provide all of the educational programming that the country needs. This assumption does not, of course, relieve the commercial broadcaster of his responsibility to serve the public interest. It does, however, recognize that certain subjects of public interest may be presented in more depth and with more continuity on stations that are not essentially commercial ventures.

The noncommercial station, like its commercial counterpart, depends to a great extent on syndicated materials. As a consequence, ETV stations are members of the National Educational Television and Radio Center, whose principal function is to supply its member ETV stations with appropriate programs on film and tape.

In addition to the ETV stations throughout the country, television has also been used for "educational" purposes in closed-circuit systems. Closed circuit means, simply, that programs are transmitted by means of cables rather than through the air. Generally, such methods of transmission are practical only at relatively short distances. A government license is not required to operate a closed-circuit system since no air waves are involved. Various schools and agencies in the United States have installed and made effective instructional use of such systems.

Instructional courses related to English and language arts curricula are presented on many of the educational stations. The pattern and objectives of these courses are similar to the courses for credit offered on commercial stations. Some of these series provide the major part of course content and are broadcast several times per week. Others are planned to enrich and supplement the presentations of the classroom teacher and are offered weekly, semimonthly, and monthly. In some communities, teachers have a choice of courses on both educational and commercial stations, for credit or not. (For example, in Philadelphia, non-credit university courses are offered on commercial station WFIL-TV, a credit course on WCAU-TV, and elementary and secondary courses on educational station WHYY-TV.)

Teachers should know the instructional television offerings in their areas in order to select and utilize the various programs with wisdom and effectiveness.

CONCLUSION

The television industry is a complicated system of "checks and balances," an interplay of instruments that sometimes are in harmony and sometimes not. The FCC has power. The advertiser has power. The stations and networks have power. Each is interested in securing the attention of the public and pleasing the public, although not always for the same reason or to the same extent. The individuals who comprise the public —in whom the ultimate power resides—in their turn are equally interested in television, a vital fact which invites us to examine television from their point of view.

CHAPTER THREE

Television and
Its Effects

In July of 1941, the Federal Communications Commission
approved commercial television. WCBW (CBS) and WNBT
(NBC), both in New York City, were the first commercially
licensed stations on the air. By the end of that year, there were
approximately 10,000 television receivers in American homes.
There was also an attack on Pearl Harbor. The networks, of
course, were forced to curtail their operations as the nation
mobilized all its resources for the war effort. The full growth
of television was thus retarded until 1948, when there were
sharp increases in the number of stations, the number of cities
served, the number of sets manufactured, and the number of
people having access to them.

Since 1948, the "fabulous infant," like any infant who
enters our home, has been unrelenting in its claims upon our
attention and highly successful in obtaining it. Television has
not only become both a conversation and furniture piece; it
has assumed the aspect of a national institution. According to
Census Bureau figures 88 per cent of the homes in the United
States display, with more or less prominence, at least one television set. Someone has noted that there are probably more
television sets in the United States than bathtubs, a probability
which invites both the enthusiastic and the cynical to make the
most of it. In any case, once the television receiver is admitted
to one's home, that home will never be quite the same. Television, to put it simply, has had an impact on our society. But
to say that any mass medium of communication exerts a social

effect is to say, after all, very little. Common sense, as well as our historical sense, permits us to assume that the individuals who compose society cannot remain indifferent to new and popular forms of communication. We may, therefore, proceed to the significant questions: To what extent and in what ways has television affected society?

There are at least two kinds of evidence that may be adduced to demonstrate the effect of television. The first is that which results from direct and controlled scientific investigation. These studies, typically, have compared groups of regular television viewers with groups that have limited or no access to television. A great many of these inquiries have dealt with the reaction of children to the heavy proportion of westerns, "private-eyes," and adventures and have attempted to answer such questions as the following: Because of "heavy exposure" to television, are children more likely to become delinquents? Do they develop unrealistic attitudes toward life's problems? Are they more passive? Are they harmfully aggressive?

> Children need a varied, well-balanced schedule of daily activities—outdoor exercise, rest, play, reading, and the warm understanding companionship of their parents. If a child is doing an excessive amount of televiewing, parents might well take a look at his daily life pattern to see how satisfying it is. Does he have varied contacts and companions, or is he turning to TV as a refuge from boredom or frustration?
>
> Since parents provide models of conduct for children, they might very well examine their own TV habits and attitudes. Some mothers may be shocked to find that they have been using TV as a baby-sitter to free themselves for other, less important responsibilities or activities.
>
> Paul Witty
> *School Children and Television*

Since a bibliography including various research studies is appended to this book, we may be synoptic here and say that there is little scientific evidence to support the hypothesis that television, by itself, is harmful to children. Dr. Joseph Klapper, formerly of the Bureau of Applied Social Research of Columbia University, has summarized his analysis of the "effects" research in all the mass media: "I think it has been pretty well demonstrated that the mass media do not serve as the primary determinant or even as a very important determinant of any of the basic attitudes or even the basic behavior patterns of either children or adults. . . ."

According to Klapper, the weight of scientific research indicates that the attitudes that make people behave the way they do are formed by forces such as the home, school, religion, and peer groups and that television tends to reinforce rather than change these attitudes. In fact, as has been suggested by Wilbur Schramm, Director of the Institute for Communication Research at Stanford University, the question, "What is television bringing to the child?" is considerably less relevant than the question, "What is the child bringing to television?" Television is, as Schramm puts it, "only one voice and one influence . . ." and, according to the scientific research, not necessarily a malignant or an overwhelming voice.

However, the scientific evidence available to us does more than simply absolve television of the sins of society. If we take the meaning of *effects* to include any kind of behavior that reveals orders of preference and habits of mind, research, particularly of the survey variety, is invariably instructive. For example, we know from one study conducted in Great Britain that children who have access to television go to bed about twenty minutes later than those who do not. From a study of the Chicago area, we learn that parents tend to watch television more hours a week than high school children do; that elementary school children watch television more than any other group, and that teachers watch least of all (in 1959 a "mere" eleven hours a week). We also know that people of all ages spend about as much time watching television today as they did when it was new.

The evidence from scientific studies can be not only instructive but frequently encouraging. For example, in the comprehensive Himmelweit study in Great Britain, *Television and the Child,* we find that television in the long run encourages children to read books, a conclusion that can be reinforced by evidence from libraries, book clubs, and publishing companies. "Book reading," Dr. Himmelweit writes, "comes into its own, not despite television but because of it."

Several observations need to be made about the kind of scientific investigation to which we have been referring. In the first place, these inquiries are dealing with short-term effects. Television has been used as a mass medium for approximately twelve years, a relatively short time for significant changes to be effected, and if effected, to be apparent. As Dr. John Bachman of the Union Theological Seminary points out in his book, *The Church in the World of Radio-Television:* "Present sociological and psychological measurements may be inadequate for tracing the deepest of attitudes, changes in which may involve years and even decades." In the second place, many of the studies, although by no means all, were designed to answer wholly negative questions. As a consequence, some important questions dealing with personal values and social attitudes remain not only unanswered but unasked. Finally, there is much disagreement in the findings of these investigations. For example, in Great Britain, although Himmelweit and her colleagues discovered that television encourages book reading, a BBC study pointed to a slight reduction in reading, and American evidence, in general, is inconclusive. These qualifications are not intended to minimize the importance of such inquiries but simply to point out some of their obvious limitations.

The second kind of evidence that may be adduced to

demonstrate the effects of television is deductive rather than inductive.

Speculation as to television's effects on our society enters into almost every conceivable aspect of behavior from *The Late Show's* effect on sleeping habits to the effect of commercials on religiosity. (Dr. Bachman notes that some children sing commercials with more enthusiasm than they do hymns.) The discussion that follows, therefore, is confined to only some of the important areas which television has touched, areas in which the teacher of English would have a special interest. If some of the comments below seem to have either the grammatical or rhetorical appearance of assertions, the reader must liberally supply his own question marks, for we are dealing here with possibilities, not certainties.

We may consider, in the first place, the effect of television on other media of communication. Radio, which was among the first to suffer from television, was not "killed" by the competition. Rather, its use and form were changed. There are in the United States today more than ten million portable radios, suggesting that radio has become a medium of mobility, of intimacy, and even of isolation. Leo Bogart in *The Age of Television* remarks that ". . . radio listening appears increasingly to be something which people do by themselves, like reading." The radio thus accompanies Americans in their automobiles and entertains them in kitchens and at beaches. Television replaces it in the living room and, of course, as the focus of family entertainment.

Similarly, the movies were forced by television to alter their previous sources of appeal. In 1946, an average of eighty-two million people attended the movies each week. By 1955, an average of only forty-six million were attending. After an initial period of uncertainty, the motion picture industry responded to television's competition by producing fewer, more expensive, and generally higher quality films.

As indicated before, evidence from surveys of the effects

of television on reading habits is contradictory. But certainly during the years of television's greatest growth, the circulation of magazines and newspapers grew and book sales soared. Reading, as I. A. Richards has said, is an antisocial activity. It is also an activity which makes powerful demands on the individual's capacity for imagination and abstraction. Watching television tends to be a collective or family activity and is frequently done in the most passive way. Apparently, reading and watching television are not only competitive but also complementary activities. On the other hand, some of the functions of reading—for example, as a means of acquiring information—are fulfilled more satisfactorily by television so that reading assumes a new role in the media spectrum. Professor Marshall McLuhan of the University of Toronto has suggested that the book, as never before, has been "elevated . . . to the role of trainer of critical and esthetic power." In other words, in learning to read we develop powers of apprehension, judgment, and selectivity which we may then apply to our experience with nonprint media.

Changes in media of communication inevitably stimulate changes in modes of education. Although courses given on closed-circuit television no doubt will ultimately affect methods of instruction, we are not here concerned with instructional television. Rather, we must consider the more profound changes that commercial television will impose on schools through its role in creating a new kind of student. For example, television provides children with an aural-visual source of information that is unprecedented in history. Long before they have learned to read or, for that matter, even begun to master their language, children may accumulate, through television, a fund of knowledge that was simply inaccessible to pre-television children. A five-year-old listening to and watching *Captain Kangeroo, Huckleberry Hound,* Walt Disney, Leonard Bernstein, or a five-minute weather report is able to learn an incredibly large number of facts, perhaps more than he can profitably assimilate. Indeed, all the technological media, of which television is but one example, expose the child to such an unrelenting stream of information that one may well ask if the "fact-centered" curriculum is not both irrelevant and confusing. Television makes possible what Margaret Mead has called "the lateral transmission" of information. By this she means the virtually instantaneous communication of ideas to every level of society, to children and adults alike. Technology may have solved the problem of getting information to people, which many still regard as the primary function of the school, thus releasing the schools to serve other purposes. Perhaps the most important of these purposes will be to teach youngsters how to make significant use of the information they can get in abundance from other sources. Facts will always be the raw material of education. But "fact-saturated" television channels may force schools to re-evaluate their traditional preoccupation with providing answers and undertake, as never before, the task of developing in students the capacity to make disciplined inquiries, sensible evaluations, and especially, to ask meaningful questions. The examination of the future may be one in which students will be asked to formulate questions rather than supply answers.

Television's effects on society go beyond those which result from its being a source of information. Television, for example, has made available on an unprecedented scale the products, both past and present, of "high culture." Adaptations of the works of Sophocles and Euripides as well as of Shaw, O'Casey, Dickens, Faulkner, Hemingway, and Henry James have been seen on network television. Almost all of Shakespeare's major plays—*King Lear, Othello, Macbeth, Hamlet, The Tempest,* to name a few—have appeared at times when millions could be expected to see and hear them. In fact, on March 11, 1956, NBC presented a three-hour broadcast of Sir Laurence Olivier's film version of *Richard III,* which was seen by one of the largest daytime audiences in television's history. Trendex surveys indicated that at least twenty-five million saw the play. If these figures are to be trusted, they mean that more people saw *Richard III* on one single afternoon than the probable combined total of audiences for stage productions of all Shakespeare's plays since he wrote them.

The most obvious deduction to which these facts lead is that we have in television an instrument of "cultural enlightenment." Great works of dramatic art which have been until recently experienced by relatively few are now projected into the homes of a great many who have by preference, insufficient motivation, or intimidation carefully avoided them. This might suggest that the general cultural level of society has been raised. There are some, however, who have argued that the availability of such programs does not in itself imply a raising of standards. Some critics have claimed that although some of the contents of television may be worthy, the undifferentiated way in which they are communicated makes it difficult for the audience to be selective and promotes a downward leveling of taste. *The Tempest* and *Gunsmoke* being packaged and presented with equal enthusiasm would, according to this view, be watched with equal passivity or, for that matter, with equal interest. The emphasis is on the "equal," not the passivity or interest.

The extent to which this inference is true points to the need for a reorientation of critical habits by the audience rather than reforms in television programming. The pages of a newspaper such as *The New York Times* or magazines such as *Life* and *Look* present to their readers a similar problem in selection and emphasis since items of unequal and unrelated significance are displayed with almost equal prominence. Although the reader is supplied with some clues of emphasis, he must, to a great extent, accentuate the page for himself. Similarly, one of the characteristics of television is that it places great burdens of selectivity on its audiences since each member of the audience cannot be confident in advance that

a particular program is intended to suit his level of sophistication.

In any case, the ultimate effect of easy access to Shakespeare and Euripides should be beneficial, especially if the
teacher of English is prepared to capitalize on their availability.

But beyond the products of "high culture" which television
makes available, what are the effects on society of the more
typical programs, the westerns, the "private-eyes," the family
shows, the adventures? Although these programs do not have
the same status or high purpose of classic literature, we may
discover, in the best of them, a "literature" that may be used
in much the same way as traditional forms have been and
are used. We may use these programs as pleasant and intelligent entertainments or diversions, as a means of increasing
our knowledge of ourselves and other people, as criticisms of
the social order, and, perhaps most important of all, as forms
which call forth satisfying aesthetic responses. The long-term
effects of television literature will ultimately depend on the
kind of viewer who watches it, and particularly, on how
selective and knowing he is in approaching that literature.

CHAPTER FOUR

The Literature of Television

For a variety of reasons, the phrase, "the literature of television," does not fall gently on the English teacher's ear. For the teacher who confines literature to written or printed forms (as the word's etymology suggests), television, by definition, cannot be properly classified as literature. For the teacher who defines literature as *belles lettres*—the higher arts of literary expression—television is excluded not only by reason of its form but by reason of its unexalted reputation. Even for the teacher whose definition of literature includes written, oral, and visual forms (so as to subsume the living theater), television's claim to the status of literature seems premature, if not presumptuous, because it cannot provide the kind of permanence we normally associate with literature. And yet, clearly, we find on television, as suggested at the close of the previous chapter, types of dramatic and narrative programs that serve many of the purposes of literature. Moreover, these programs possess at least some of the distinguishing traits of literature. For if we recognize, as Wellek and Warren do, that fiction, invention, and imagination are characteristics of literary form, then we must concede that these characteristics may be found as abundantly in certain television programs as in certain books. For our purposes then, the word *literature* is used metaphorically and as a description, not as an evaluation. We do not mean to suggest by its use that television is the equivalent of *belles lettres* but rather that certain kinds of

> . . . I run into people who seem to feel that literature is all words and that words should preferably be a little stuffy. Who knows what literature is? The literature of the Cro Magnon is painted on the walls of the caves of Altamira. Who knows but that the literature of the future will be projected on clouds? Our present argument that literature is the written and printed word in poetry, drama, and the novel has no very eternal basis in fact. Such literature has not been with us very long, and there is nothing to indicate that it will continue with us for very long (at least the way it is going). If people don't read it, it just isn't going to be literature.
>
> John Steinbeck
> Introduction to *The World of Li'l Abner*

television programs employ language and action in ways that duplicate the functions of traditional literary forms. Using words and images, television can, for example, tell stories— long, short, serious, or comic ones—in narration or dramatization. In using the phrase, "the literature of television," therefore, we are referring to those types of programs analogous in many of their purposes, if not in their form, to novels, short stories, plays, even essays. Before examining these types of programs in detail (we have called them "genres"), let us consider, in general, some of the similarities and differences between the literature of television and the more traditional forms with which we are all familiar.

Like all literary types, the literature of television reflects the assumptions and values of the men who create it and, to some extent, their assumptions about the audiences for whom they create. Thus, if there were few television plays of "social protest" in the 1950's, neither in literature nor in society were there many powerful and sustained expressions of social protest during the same period. Although we may criticize some of the literature of television for encouraging the acquisition of material comforts as an end in itself, we must concede that this tendency, too, is a genuine reflection of our times rather than an emphasis manufactured by latter-day Medicis. No doubt some of our collective virtues have also been reflected in the literature of television, as for example, our growing awareness of the dangers of class prejudice and ethnic stereotypes. In other words, to the extent that we may trust literature to reveal the prevailing attitudes of an era, television is perhaps as useful an index of the last decade as any other form of literature.

A second similarity is that, like the novel, short story, or play, the literature of television is uneven in quality. At its best, it is truthful and artistic. At its worst, it is trivial and formless. This is not to suggest that the best of television, say, Paddy Chayefsky's *Marty,* is the artistic equivalent of the best of twenty-four hundred years of the theater or even four hundred years of the novel. Such comparisons are unjust as well as unproductive. Rather, we are suggesting that in television, as in other literary forms, there are levels of value. *The Death of a Salesman* is a far cry from *Abie's Irish Rose* but perhaps no farther than is television's *Requiem for a Heavyweight* from *This Is Your Life.*

The literature of television is created within certain limitations, limitations imposed by the form of the medium. Limitations of form are, of course, well known to creators of novels, short stories, poems, journalism, stage plays, and films. The nature and extent of these limitations as they apply specifically to any medium define that medium's difference from other forms. For example, the form of the novel may be flexible enough to integrate, even exploit, lengthy philosophic discourse. The form of the film is not. The film, however, through the process of editing, lends itself to striking manipulations of time and space, while on "live" television such manipulations are less effective. The narrator may serve as a useful, perhaps essential, dramatic device on radio. In the theater, the Greek Chorus of *Electra* and the stage manager of *Our Town* notwithstanding, the narrator is less believable or, at least, less conventional.

The main part of this chapter will deal directly with the technical and artistic limitations and resources that make television unique. But some important differences between television and others forms of literature need mentioning before we begin.

In the first place, since the literature of television is transmitted simultaneously to millions of people, its creators are subject to limitations of theme, language, and style more severe than those in other media. In general, the wider the base of the audience, the greater the degree of restriction imposed on the creator, and no contemporary literary form has a more heterogeneous or massive audience than television.

In the second place, the line that separates commercial interests from literary interests in television is less distinct than in most other literary forms. To be sure, the publisher of novels and the producer of stage plays are concerned with making money. But in television, as we have tried to indicate in Chapter Two, the advertiser, the man who pays the bills, is primarily concerned with the sale of a commercial product rather than an artistic one. At the same time, selling products and presenting high quality programs are not necessarily incompatible motives. There are, in fact, numerous examples of sponsors who have done both simultaneously.

Teachers must remember, too, that the literature of television, unlike most types of literature, is highly ephemeral in character. At the moment, the libraries of television are its "reruns," but even so, a particular show must be seen at a specific time or it cannot be seen at all. As a result, studying or teaching about television presents certain problems not found in the study of other types of literature, except the legitimate stage.

Finally, unlike most types of literature, the literature of television defies easy classification. This poses a problem not only for those who would study or teach it but even for those who would praise it. For example, in 1948, when the National Academy of Television Arts and Sciences presented its first "Emmys," five awards were given, one of which was for "Best Film for Television" and another for "Most Popular Television Program." The following year, neither of these categories was represented even though nine awards were given.

As the number of different types of programs increased through the years, the problem of establishing recognizable "genres" became more difficult. A humorous example of the unwieldy proportions of the problem was provided in 1957 when an award was given for the "Best Continuing Perform-ance (Male) in a Series by a Comedian, Singer, Host, Dancer, M.C., Announcer, Narrator, Panelist, or Any Person Who Essentially Plays Himself." Although this extraordinary award was never repeated, its appearance—even once—suggests the difficulties involved in classifying television programs. Clearly, any coherent treatment of the literature of television must necessarily be selective. Since the purpose of this chapter is to provide the reader with a sense of the significance of what we are calling *the literature of television,* the following dis-cussions are concerned only with those types of television pro-grams which have distinguished themselves by virtue of artis-tic quality, by reason of their unfailing popularity, or by the clarity with which they express social values.

ORIGINAL TELEVISION DRAMA

In his book, *The Public Arts,* Gilbert Seldes uses the term the *fifty-two-minute hour* to refer to a popular dramatic form which began and matured between the years 1948 and 1958. Approximately 1500 fifty-two-minute plays were per-formed "live" during those ten years. The term *live* refers, of course, to the fact that these plays were performed at the pre-cise moment that they were seen by the television audience, a condition which since the advent of videotape has become increasingly rare; "fifty-two minutes" describes the actual running time of the play, eight minutes of the hour being subtracted for commercial messages, the listing of credits, and publicity for next week's play.

Undoubtedly, some of television's finest moments were provided by these fifty-two minute hours, particularly by such weekly series as *The Kraft Television Theater* (1947-1958), *The Philco-Goodyear Playhouse* (1948-1955), and *Studio One* (1948-1957). These programs began by presenting adaptations of the classics and established contemporary novels but by 1950 shifted their emphasis from adaptations to "originals." By that time, such producers and directors as Worthington Miner, Fred Coe, Delbert Mann, Arthur Penn, and John Frankenheimer had assembled about them several gifted, young writers who were prepared to devote their collective talents to a serious exploration of television's artistic resources. Included in that group, among others, were Reginald Rose, Tad Mosel, Robert Alan Aurthur, Horton Foote, Rod Serling, J. P. Miller, and Gore Vidal. None, however, wrote more fittingly for television than Paddy Chayefsky.

Chayefsky was to the "original" television drama what Ibsen was to the "social drama," which is to say that he was one of its first creators and certainly its most distinguished one. And, like Ibsen, he achieved an almost perfect union of form and content. Critics have observed, for example, that the effects that Ibsen achieved in *A Doll's House* and *Ghosts* were a function not of his themes alone, with which audiences were certainly familiar in 1879 and 1881, but a result of the stark, simple, and economical form in which he stated his themes. Social dramas had been written before Ibsen, but it remained for him to discover the proper form for dramatizing social problems.

Chayefsky, however, did not write for the proscenium arch which is viewed from a distance in a darkened theater.

He wrote for a seventeen-inch screen which was situated in the family living room and on which the only colors were varying shades of grey. He also had to present his story, from start to finish, in fifty-two minutes and could make two assumptions with almost absolute assurance. The first was that his play would be interrupted at least twice for commercial messages. The second was that he would have to attract his audience instantly or lose much of it to other channels. He knew, too, as did his director, Delbert Mann, that the picture on the television screen is considerably cruder in its visual definition than that of the motion picture screen. Thus, Chayefsky wrote his plays in anticipation of the audience's observing the players in almost unrelenting "close-up."

Chayefsky realized that some of these unique technical-aesthetic conditions could create, as perhaps no other medium, a sense of utter and absolute reality, could create the illusion that what the audience was watching was not a mere play but life as seen through a seventeen-inch, nearly square hole. Beginning with *Holiday Song,* which dealt with a rabbi's re-examination of his faith in God, Chayefsky created a series of distinguished dramas that have often been characterized as "small" masterpieces. They were plays about unexceptional people who existed for fifty-two minutes in wholly unexceptional situations. The plots were uncluttered, undaring, and highly compressed. They had few unexpected turns, little action, no treachery, no perversion, and no heroic gestures (in a traditional sense). Chayefsky's stories were "small" in very much the same way that Sherwood Anderson's stories were small. The setting was the Bronx, not small-town Ohio, and Chayefsky was less concerned than was Anderson with "social outcasts." But, like Anderson, Chayefsky explored in economical but meticulous detail the agonizing problems of small people, thus elevating the status of both the problems and the people who suffered them. In fact, Chayefsky has said that "your mother, sister, brothers, cousins, friends—all of these are better subjects for drama than Iago." He was talking, of course, about television drama.

Chayefsky's most widely known play, *Marty,* tells the story of an unmarried and inarticulate Bronx butcher who is attracted to a sensitive but homely girl. Marty's friends attempt to dissuade him from seeing the girl because she is, in their words, "a dog." His mother, who fears being abandoned, resents the girl. Against a backdrop of such universal themes as man's need of loving and being loved, his fear of living alone, and his need of communicating articulately, Chayefsky pursues a "small" story with a persistent literalness, concluding with an equally "small" crisis in which Marty decides, against the protest of his friends and family, to phone the girl and ask her for a date. On the stage or in novel form, the plot alone would probably be too flimsy to carry much dramatic weight. When the play was adapted for the movies, it required more "movement" or action and the addition of at least one subplot. On the television screen, however, the play was an artistic masterpiece, producing an illusion of intimacy that was at once disturbing and edifying. Perhaps no other medium is better suited to the "slice of life" drama than television, and Chayefsky exploited this fact repeatedly.

Chayefsky was not alone in exploring the unique qualities of the television screen, but some of the other writers did not place the same emphasis as he on the explication, in naturalistic terms, of the problems of ordinary people. Reginald Rose, for example, favored the "message" play, such as *Twelve Angry Men* and *Tragedy in a Temporary Town,* in which he exhorted his audience to discard its prejudices. Gore Vidal wrote television's most literate satire, *Visit to a Small Planet,* which in simulated Shavian style condemned man's most persistent talent, the making of war. Rod Serling examined the motivations and pressures of "big business" in his highly successful *Patterns.* And Alvin Sapinsley experimented with poetic dramas, one of which, *Lee at Gettysburg,* was suggestive in its rhythm and compression, of the poetic dramas of radio.

Whatever differences existed among these various writers, the success of each may be attributed to his ability to recognize certain inescapable facts about the medium, its audience, and the environment in which the audience characteristically viewed his play. For example, television drama seems to be singularly effective when focused on people rather than plots, places, or even ideas. As mentioned before, the "normal" view of the players on the television screen is the "close-up." As a consequence, the human face is given such continued and forceful presence that it tends to become the overriding emphasis of the play, whether the author intends it or not. Bridges falling down and planes zooming high may be thrillingly pictured in films and novels. On live television, the space limitations of a studio make such actions technically impractical, if not impossible. Even in film sequences, such actions are not as dramatically persuasive because of the smallness of the screen and the relatively crude definition of the image. Television, as one director put it, is the "psychoanalytic medium." What television drama does best is to show faces and to suggest what is behind them. Of this quality, Rod Serling wrote, "The key to TV drama was intimacy, and the facial study on a small screen carried with it a meaning and power far beyond its usage in the motion pictures."

Also, television drama must be highly compressed. There is little time for subplots or for much elaboration of even the main plot. The television dramatist, like the short story writer, has time only to relate a bare narrative and evoke a mood. Of course, unlike the short story writer, he has the camera to help him do both. Occasionally, as we will demonstrate in our discussion of the adaptation of "The Killers" (in Part Two), the television writer is faced with the problem of expanding a brief story, but, typically, his problem is the reverse. "Television," Paddy Chayefsky wrote, "cannot take a thick, fully woven fabric of drama. It can only handle simple lines of movement and consequently smaller moments of crisis."

We must remember also that television is family entertainment viewed within the home. This tends to impose limitations on both the language and the themes of television plays. Nymphomania, homosexuality, or incest may be maturely explored in the theater and in other literary forms, but on television such subjects tend to be shocking, not only because of television's unselected audience but especially because

References to religion are generally treated with great caution on all programs. Many critics feel that too much caution is exercised and that the medium should present differences between faiths soberly, while avoiding controversy. But even in England, with its tradition of public debate of religious issues, atheist lecturer Margaret Knight's 1955 BBC programs on "Morals without Religion" drew many letters of complaint. In America an example of the kind of fuss generated by religious matters was when Garry Moore announced that he would give St. Christopher's medals to his staff. Moore, who is an Episcopalian, was accused of hypocrisy by viewers who thought he was Jewish and of favoritism by those who thought he was Catholic. Another ferment was created when a Chicago local station withdrew its plans to premiere the film *Martin Luther* in 1956, amidst charges of censorship. Another Chicago station WBKB, showed the film, without incident, a few months later. On the other hand, a drama like *The Little Moon of Alban* showed a complex religious theme could be handled with good taste and effectiveness, and it drew praise from both critics and audience.

Charles Winick
Taste and the Censor in Television

of the almost painful explicitness of the medium. "It is far worse," writes Jan Bussell in *The Art of Television*, "to see someone spewing in your sitting room than hear it only." Or, one might add, than to see it in a darkened theater. Similarly, words which would scarcely be remembered when read in novels or heard on the stage can almost never be forgotten when they invade the living room. A now famous example of this fact occurred on February 19, 1956, at which time *The Alcoa Hour* presented Reginald Rose's *Tragedy in a Temporary Town*. One of the actors, Lloyd Bridges, was overcome by the excitement of a particular scene and uttered an expletive that was not in the script but which might have been had the play been performed on the stage. The words themselves would have gone practically unnoticed in a Norman Mailer or Nelson Algren novel. On television, the event was a *cause célèbre*. (No connection exists between this incident and the fact that Lloyd Bridges now appears on television under water with an oxygen mask tightly covering his mouth.)

Television writers worked for years within these limitations and produced a substantial body of serious drama. But for various reasons, the fifty-two minute live drama has become increasingly rare. In the first place, some writers abandoned television altogether because they felt it did not provide sufficient artistic freedom or financial reward. They objected, for example, to the intrusion of commercial messages and to the imposition of thematic limitations by sponsors. And, of course, they have found that writing for the movies is far more lucrative.

In the second place, many producers abandoned the fifty-two minute hour because a weekly series demanded a constant source of talent that was simply not available. Television is a ravenous consumer of talent and material. It must be fed eighteen hours a day, seven days a week. The most gifted find it difficult to survive such a relentless challenge of their creative resources. Even if Paddy Chayefsky, Tad Mosel, J. P. Miller, and all the others were still writing for television, they probably could not produce distinguished hour-long dramas week after week. Finally, many sponsors abandoned the form because it was more expensive than filmed half-hour shows and not quite as magnetic as the ninety-minute or two-hour "special."

Nevertheless, high quality, "original" drama still exists on television. Reginald Rose and Robert Alan Aurthur write less frequently for television now but are still concerned with it. Rod Serling has turned his attention to the thirty-minute filmed drama in a series called *The Twilight Zone*. *The Hallmark Hall of Fame* and the *Armstrong Circle Theater* have been distinguished for the high quality of their dramas, although the first has emphasized adaptations and the last, semi-documentaries. In addition, gifted new writers have continued to explore the medium in the serious tradition of their predecessors. James Costigan's *Little Moon of Alban,* Alfred Brenner's *Survival* (on the *United States Steel Hour*), and Alvin Boretz's work on the *Armstrong Circle Theater,* among others, suggest that "original" television drama will continue to make an important contribution to American literature.

Moreover, the advent of videotape has given great impetus to the development of an "elite" theater, that is, television drama aimed at special audiences. Such programs as *The Play of the Week, The Robert Herridge Theater,* and *Camera Three* may be seen, on tape, in many cities throughout the country. *The Play of the Week* has been particularly distinguished for its adaptations of classics, such as *Medea, Don Juan in Hell, Tiger at the Gates, The Cherry Orchard*, and *The Iceman Cometh.*

In addition to its efforts to present original and serious dramatic programs, television has provided its audiences with an abundance of fiction which, although largely stereotyped in form and in spirit, may fairly be regarded as an important part of television's literature, certainly in terms of popularity. We are referring to westerns, "cops and robbers," and family programs. We call these three types of fiction "genres" because each is a special kind of television literature, possessing a style, form, and purpose that distinguishes it from other types of television fiction.

THE WESTERN

There is an understandable impression among the young of the land that the western is synonymous with television itself. In actual fact, the western did not fully emerge on television until 1955, or approximately seven years after commercial television started nationwide operations. The earliest television westerns—*Hopalong Cassidy, Roy Rogers,* and *The Lone Ranger*—were imported creations from the movies and radio, and were, for the most part, popular only with children. On September 6, 1955, the ABC Television Network introduced Wyatt Earp in an "adult" western, and several evenings later, the CBS Television Network featured another one, *Gunsmoke* (in point of fact, an import from radio). From that month on the western has probably been the most popular literary "genre" on television.

As indicated above, the western did not, as Minerva from Jove's head, spring full grown from the television screen or, for that matter, from the movie screen. On the contrary, the western has been a fully developed mythology for probably close to one hundred years. Its earliest outlines may be identified, for one example, in James Fenimore Cooper's five Leatherstocking Tales, the second of which, *The Last of the Mohicans,* has sold more than two million copies in America alone. Since the frontier did not extend much beyond the Mississippi River when Cooper wrote, the setting of his "easterns" is upper New York State in the latter half of the eighteenth century and not the Southwest in the second half of the nineteenth. But differences in time and place do not obscure similarities of spirit and invention. For example, Cooper insisted that he was writing history, not fiction. In the preface of his first edition of *The Last of the Mohicans,* published in 1826, he wrote, "The reader, who takes up these volumes, in expectation of finding an imaginary and romantic picture of things which never happened, will probably lay them aside, disappointed."

In spite of this disclaimer, Cooper's stories have little enough to do with the realities of life in the wilderness. Cooper wrote pure romances in the guise of history, and in this he set a pattern which was emulated by later writers of frontier tales. Owen Wister, for example, claimed that his *The Virginian,* published in 1902, was a historical novel of the cattle country. But, as Frank Luther Mott has observed, there is not one cow in the entire book. Similarly, modern-day westerns (whether in novel, film, or television form) claim, at least by implication, to possess a certain degree of verisimilitude. However, historians find little resemblance between their fictions and the literal facts. Cattle, for example, play only an incidental part in the modern western. The main and even minor characters rarely engage in the kind of strenuous labor that dominated the growth of the frontier. And heroes who are supposed to be modeled after men who actually lived bear little relation to their real life counterparts. For example, historical evidence indicates that the actual Wild Bill Hickok, Wyatt Earp, Bat Masterson, and Billy the Kid possessed qualities and performed deeds that were considerably less than admirable. Nevertheless, out of this unpromising material, magazines, newspapers, novels, and films fashioned extraordinary "culture heroes," heroes not unlike Cooper's Natty Bumppo. Bumppo preferred the company of men, idealized women, and performed feats that are patently impossible, as Mark Twain clearly demonstrated in his essay on Cooper's literary offenses. He was also virtuous, pious, and almost always correct. These qualities are certainly to be found in our modern cowboys. None, to be sure, can shoot quite so well as Bumppo, who could hit a nailhead at a distance of 100 yards; but generally in skill, motivation, and attitude, the cowboy is clearly a distant relative of Leatherstocking.

A weekly publication, *The National Police Gazette,* is frequently cited as having been one of the original manufacturers of the legendary cowboy, at least as he exists in his present form. Perhaps the prototype is more directly found in Bret Harte's stories of western mining towns, complete with brawls, romances, and hold-ups. Whatever their original source, the legends of the West apparently fascinate Americans and, quite naturally, have been given form on television.

The television western has, for the most part, maintained the spirit of the tradition. In other words, television continues to present the western as the most unsubtle of all modern morality plays. The characters in a typical television western are clearly the embodiments of various virtues and vices. There is, for example, the Good Guy, the Bad Guy, and even the Grey Guy. (According to John Steinbeck, the Grey Guy is one who may start out good and end up bad or start out bad and end up good.) As in the less sophisticated morality play, the symbols of virtue and vice must not only be unambiguous but immediately recognizable. The Good Guy, in general, wears a light hat and clean light clothes (particularly if he is a law man). He knows no fear, is facile with some deadly weapon, and is as courteous to women as he is indifferent to their sexuality. He is tall and handsome and, usually, is not much of a conversationalist. He is rarely troubled by moral ambiguities and is, of course, never called upon to make decisions that involve complex rational processes. In each play, Good is clearly distinguished from Evil, although people of sensibility will easily discern flaws in the dichotomy. For example, frequently the Good Guy defends the Good in questionable ways and thus tarnishes the virtue of his cause. Also, occasionally, the Good Guy equates mere petulance with Evil, dealing with those who are only sources of irritation as if they were serious advocates of the Devil.

Each hero usually has some personal symbol which distinguishes him from all similar types. Paladin (*Have Gun,*

Will Travel) distributes at appropriate moments a simple business card which states his name, address, and occupation. Josh Randall (*Wanted: Dead or Alive*) carries in an over-sized holster what surely must be the biggest pistol ever manu-factured. Tate (*Tate*) has the use of only one arm. Bat Masterson has the use of three, if one counts his all-purpose cane.

The Bad Guy, like the Good Guy, is also enveloped in stock symbols. The Bad Guy may be defined as a man who smokes cigarettes or cigars, is unshaved and unclean, wears black hats, and is the second "fastest gun in town."

Television, as have the novel and the film, has provided some notable departures from these stock characters and simple allegories. In *The Ox-Bow Incident,* for example, Walter Van Tilburg Clark used a western setting in which to probe deeply into the nature of guilt and man's inhumanity to man. Clark's characters—true to the western tradition— are clearly allegorical, but in providing them with complex and entirely believable motivations, he elevated his story to the status of tragedy. Similarly, the film, *High Noon,* although using the standard materials of the formula western, achieved something approaching artistic distinction by its development of characters who react fearfully but humanly to the con-frontation of Evil. On television, departures from the formula western have largely taken the form of parody rather than tragedy. In *Have Gun, Will Travel,* the Good Guy is almost a direct refutation of his entire breed. He is materialistic (as a professional gunfighter, he invariably demands payment in advance), sensual (at the beginning of a typical play, he is on the verge of making love to a beautiful woman), and literate (in one show, he out-talked, of all people, Oscar Wilde). But the best example of the parody-western may be found in *Maverick.* Maverick is the family name of two brothers who at first appearance seem to be typical Good Guys. They are handsome, tall, and wear the standard symbols of justice, guns. But beyond this superficial resemblance they are the exact opposite of Matt Dillon of *Gunsmoke* or Wyatt Earp. The brothers Maverick are, in fact, frequently cowardly, conventionally interested in women, and by occupation and temperament, professional gamblers. The tone of the program is invariably breezy, and its intention is clearly to poke fun at the entire "genre." *Maverick,* in short, approaches literary criticism, as parody always does.

Perhaps the best explanation of the wide appeal of the formula western may be found in the psychological needs of the audience. The western's clear moral imperatives, its emphasis on raw physical danger rather than the insecurities of a modern society, its overt rather than suppressed violence, and its evocation of a mythical, but romantic, past no doubt touch something that runs deep in American culture. The western appears to fill a need that in other times for other people may have been satisfied by tales of gallant knights and fair damsels in distress.

Many people have objected to the degree to which violence is depicted on westerns and other "action" programs. Of course, almost by definition, there must be *some* physical contact on an "action" program. The question is whether or not all the shootings or fights are artistically essential to plot or character development. Both industry and citizen pressures have been exerted in behalf of less violence in general and of no "unnecessary" violence in particular. But since the question of what is or is not necessary to a story involves a subjective judgment, the problem is not easily resolved. Certainly, this is a matter to which teachers ought to give careful thought. Apparently, there is no end in sight to the western, even though its lack of variety suggests that the saturation point may have been reached. Perhaps in the immediate years ahead the romantic legends of the West will be replaced by adventures of space travel. Outer space is, after all, the new frontier.

COPS AND ROBBERS

Like the western the "cops and robbers" story that is so ubiquitous on television has a history many years older than television itself. The theme has been explored with creative variety in novels, short stories, and films. In fact, early formulations of this motif date as far back as the fifteenth century when tales of Robin Hood and his relentless pursuer, the Sheriff of Nottingham, took form in poems and ritual dramas. The Robin Hood legends, however, are more properly described as "robbers and cops" stories, since it is the outlaw, not the law officer, who is the object of admiration and emulation. Despite Hollywood's protestations to the contrary, the "gangster" movies of the 1930's were very much in this tradition. Like Robin's discontented band of Saxons, James Cagney's "mob" of public enemies lived romantic, violent, and episodic lives, lives which were largely free from the customary restraints and proscriptions imposed by society. Possibly fifteenth-century Britons, as well as twentieth-century Americans, found these tales appealing precisely because they admired the courage and ingenuity that is required to survive in such a wildly antisocial manner. We may, however, infer important differences between the values of the fifteenth-century Britons and twentieth-century Americans by attending to the manner in which their robber-hero concluded his career. Robin Hood was ultimately pardoned by King Richard I, and thus the outlaw's unconventional style of life was justified. James Cagney (or Paul Muni-Edward G. Robinson) was ultimately mutilated by machine-gun fire, and the audience's conventional style of life was justified.

The television "cops and robbers" story comes in two varieties, both of which are from more recent literary stock than fifteenth-century legends. In fact, both are probably direct descendants of the Sherlock Holmes stories, which is to say, among other things, that the audience's sympathies are enlisted on the side of the detective, not the criminal. Occasionally, in, say, *The Untouchables,* a gangster's breezy disregard of our legal apparatus will perversely engage our admiration, just as, occasionally, Professor Moriarty's resourcefulness commands our affection. But for the most part, the television "cops and robbers" story is focused on the detective and his problems and has a high moral tone.

One of the varieties of television detective literature may be described as being in the "romantic" mode and the other, in the "realistic." Let us consider the romantic first.

Sometimes the romantic detective-hero is a semi-official officer of the law, such as the lawyer Perry Mason. But typically, he is a "private-eye," that is, a self-employed detective whose relation to official legal apparatus is largely informal and frequently antagonistic. Like Holmes, he is a bachelor, possesses an inexhaustible fund of potentially valuable information, and has his own unconventional methods of detection. He also has a friendly but patronizing attitude toward all police officers (for example, Lt. Tragg plays Inspector Lestrade to Perry Mason's Holmes). Like Holmes, some television "private-eyes" are attended by a faithful and ever-admiring friend who appears to have no interests in life other than to pay homage to his companion.

In *77 Sunset Strip,* a frivolous parking-lot attendant—appropriately named Kookie—plays Dr. Watson to Stuart Bailey's Holmes. While Kookie is not nearly so ingenuous as Watson, Watson would undoubtedly be startled by Kookie's lack of taste and education. Moreover, Kookie is rarely as useful as Watson. We may infer important differences between nineteenth-century England and twentieth-century America by attending to the differences in character between Watson and Kookie. The character of Kookie is undoubtedly a concession to the audience's demonstrated taste for well-proportioned and inarticulate heroes, a type that would scarcely be of interest to a Victorian audience. Watson, as well as the chronicler of Monsieur Dupin's adventures, is a mature, literate, and fairly well-informed companion. This difference notwithstanding, both Kookie and Watson serve the same dramatic role—"straight men" who occasionally can be the source of comic relief.

In spite of certain resemblances to Holmes, the modern private-eye has unique characteristics. Holmes was, after all, a Victorian. The private-eye is a reflection of more recently established social values and patterns of behavior. He actively eyes unattached women, rarely expresses surprise or indignation over grotesque crimes, and probably would find violin playing an absurd avocation. Also, unlike Holmes', his powers of observation are hardly impressive, and he employs only the most rudimentary logic in solving crimes, sometimes blundering his way to their solutions. Whereas Holmes is successful because he is cleverer than the criminal he pursues, Stuart Bailey of 77 Sunset Strip succeeds because the criminal is stupider than he. Also, Holmes is seldom violent, which of course distinguishes him sharply from those television detectives who have been patterned after types originally found in Raymond Chandler and Dashiell Hammett novels.

And yet, in spite of his blunted sensibilities, the private-eye frequently emerges as a romantic figure. In his own way, he is sophisticated, winsome, unpredictable, well paid, and haphazardly effective. He is also pure myth. Real life private detectives do not normally engage in the kind of work their television counterparts are weekly called upon to do, and might be terrified at the prospect. In short, the private-eye is almost the direct opposite of the realistic Sgt. Joe Friday of Dragnet, who along with his imitators, represents television's most original variation of the "cops and robbers" theme.

Sgt. Joe Friday was created by Jack Webb, who, in 1952, after several successful years on radio, brought his program, Dragnet, to television. Using conventional cinematic and radio techniques, but with important modifications for the purposes of television, Webb achieved an impressive illusion of reality that opened new possibilities to "cops and robbers" literature. With the exception of its standard opening—a long shot view of the City of Los Angeles—almost the entire program was shot in "close-up." Webb was only minimally concerned with the supposedly dramatic ways in which criminals are apprehended. Instead, he focused the audience's attention on the process of interrogation, emphasizing the inherent drama in simple questions and answers by frequently and sequentially cutting from one face to another. Approximately half of the program's dialogue (or so it seemed) consisted of terse questions and guarded answers. Most of the performers on the show were "fresh faces," many of whom pretended to be as uncertain about their own performances as they were about their answers to Friday's questions.

Sgt. Friday, played by Webb himself, functioned also as the narrator of *Dragnet,* addressing the audience in tired, clipped, official, and sometimes technical language. Whether in the role of narrator or detective-hero, Friday was invariably grim and coldly efficient, the embodiment of all the impersonal mechanisms of law enforcement. He did not seek the audience's sympathy or friendship, only its attention. True to the Holmes tradition, Friday was provided with a kindly companion who softened his almost unbelievable dedication to work. But Friday was Holmesian only in the sense that he unfailingly solved his case. Unlike Holmes, Friday did not achieve success through imagination, logic, and daring. Friday appeared to be a cop, a "real cop," his success being a result of hard work and the backing of an efficient scientific machinery, the Los Angeles Police Force.

There are, of course, no cops exactly like Joe Friday, and it is a tribute to Webb's artistry that he was able to convince millions that there are. Nevertheless, with its concern for verisimilitude and its representation (even if stylized) of things "as they really are," *Dragnet* was in the tradition of the realistic movement in literature. Its final season on network television was in 1958, but *Dragnet* set a pattern which has been emulated, with varying degrees of success, by *The Line-up*, *Naked City*, *M-Squad*, and *The Untouchables*. In fact, *The Untouchables* has gone even further than *Dragnet* in its efforts at realism. Each *Dragnet* program began with the ominous information that the "story you are about to see is true. Only the names have been changed, to protect the innocent." In *The Untouchables*, real names are used (for example, Al Capone) and the narrator, Walter Winchell, reports the events of the story much as if he were reporting events on one of his news programs. The enormous popularity of this program is a measure of the convincing manner in which it tells an old story.

THE FAMILY SHOW

On television, family life is largely a laughing matter. At least there is no example in the history of television of a weekly program which dealt with the experiences of a family in anything but comic fashion. Occasionally, in the more successful programs, such as *The Goldbergs* and *Mama* (which were originally created in other media), the family would confront situations that were more serious than funny. But for the most part, family programs are classified as "situation comedies."

The Goldbergs and *Mama* are notable for two other reasons. They were the first family programs on television, both coming in 1949 (*The Goldbergs* in January, *Mama* in July). And they were clearly "ethnic" family stories, a genre within a genre. *The Goldbergs*, for example, derived much of its humor from the fact that the Goldbergs were a Jewish family living in The Bronx. Just as Leo Rosten's Hyman Kaplan would be pointless and certainly not funny if he were not an immigrant Jew, Uncle David and Molly herself were comprehensible only in terms of a specific cultural and religious context. In their last days on television, the Goldbergs were transplanted to a small suburban town, where, fortunately, they did not last long. Molly and Uncle David were as irrelevant in suburbia as Wyatt Earp would be on Broadway and 42nd Street.

The family programs that followed *The Goldbergs* and *Mama* did not emulate them. The Andersons (*Father Knows Best*), Rileys (*Life of Riley*), Nelsons (*The Adventures of Ozzie and Harriet*), Stevens (*I Married Joan*), and the Henshaws (*December Bride*) have no specific religious or subcultural identification unless it is of a vague, white, middle-class nature.

The reasons for the absence of ethnic stories in current family programs are not hard to find. In the first place, with the exception of the Puerto Rican migration, there have been no new cultural strains assimilated into American life for many years. (Indeed, the only recent family show in which there was an element of a "foreign" culture was *I Love Lucy,* Ricky Ricardo being a Cuban.) Presumably, the adult sons and daughters of immigrant Jews, Swedes, Italians, Poles, Russians, Greeks, Germans, and Irish think of themselves as "Americans" more than as members of a particular subgroup. Thus, they might find ethnic stories more strange than wonderful. In the second place, the wide base of television's audience tends to induce writers to create characters who have something in common with each viewer. This seems to require that characters not possess any quality that might suggest an identification with a particular group. Thus, although we might assume that Chester Riley is of Irish background and Jim Anderson of Swedish, no evidence other than their names confirms this. Ironically, one show which did maintain an ethnic quality, *Amos 'n' Andy,* was frequently accused of perpetuating a grotesque stereotype.

Real families, of course, are identified by more than their

religious or cultural backgrounds. They have political biases. Television families have no political preferences, unless by excluding politics from their lives, they do, in fact, make a political gesture. In any case, the families depicted on television remain largely indifferent to any of the larger social and political issues with which most of the audience is familiar. Here again, the explanation is probably to be found in the wide base of the audience, segments of which would undoubtedly feel betrayed if Jim Anderson turned out to be an active member of either the Democratic or Republican party.

Real families, also, find themselves as members of a particular economic class. Some are rich, some are poor, and some, neither. Television families appear to be, almost uniformly, in the last group. With the possible exception of the McCoys in *The Real McCoys,* television families are characteristically surrounded by the symbols of middle-class life in America. The television family is "well fixed," but not so "well fixed" as to offend any members of the audience who might still be struggling to make a living. The Chinese house-boy in *Bachelor Father* is perhaps the only clear-cut symbol of high income in a television family.

In short, the American family as it is portrayed on television is as Norman Rockwell, or perhaps DeWitt Wallace of *Reader's Digest,* claims to see it. It consists of a father and mother and some handsome and "nervy" children. It functions in a house, a school, and an automobile in the "low-priced field." It faces problems, to be sure, but none that are essentially serious and none that cannot be solved through the application of simple good will. And, of course, everything is entirely above board. Jim Anderson would no sooner "fix" a traffic ticket or give himself an advantage on his income tax returns than Matt Dillon would refuse to draw against an evil killer. In other words, the family show, like the western and "cops-and-robbers" programs, is a romance.

Romances, of course, are not expected to be true in the

sense of their depicting what actually exists. In our frontier history, we find no such character as Paladin, the gunfighter. In our police history, we find no such policeman as television's Eliot Ness. In our society, we find no such family as the Andersons. What "truth" there is in a romance must be an artistic truth, not a literal one. Cooper's Bumppo, Poe's Dupin, Doyle's Holmes, Tarkington's William Baxter, even Mark Twain's Huck Finn are true only in the sense of their having a convincing artistic reality. Paladin, Eliot Ness, and Jim Anderson convey to millions a similar truth. In addition, their actions express values which the audience finds at least theoretically congenial. Jim Anderson of *Father Knows Best,* for example, is honest, sympathetic, and genteel in an unaffected way. He gets along well with others. He is a man whose convictions will never place him in danger of losing friends, money, or status in the community. He seems to be educated, but he is not an "egghead." He is the head of his household, but he rules it gently. He wears a smoking jacket in the living room and pajamas in bed, and when roused from sleep he is invariably well groomed and instantly articulate. If he does not exist, at least we can say of him that millions wish he did.

THE ACTUALITY NARRATIVE

Although westerns, "cops and robbers," and family stories form an important part of television's literary stock in trade, these types of programs are not, in the purest sense, native to television. First, these are themes that were developed in other media long before they were brought to the television screen. But even more important, such programs, almost without variation, are on film, many of them having been produced in Hollywood. They are essentially twenty-six- or fifty-two-minute movies that are seen on a television set rather than a movie screen. Of course, in the production of these films important modifications are made to accommodate some of the unique conditions imposed by the television screen. For example, there are many more close-ups than are normally used in films shown in theaters. Long shots are rarely used. More dialogue is needed. The casts tend to be smaller, and much less attention is paid to lighting since subtle contrasts of black and white will go unnoticed on a small, grey television screen.

Yet film and television are by no means identical communication forms. A movie involves the taking of pictures, pictures which, in the first place, must be developed in a laboratory, and, in the second place, may be arranged and then projected in almost any order a director or editor wishes. Thus, the film director may give to an audience an artfully manufactured sense of time and space. He may, for example, compress time, expand it, or even create the illusion of simultaneity. A typical movie technique for achieving suspense involves alternately projecting different shots onto the screen so as to create the impression that, for instance, a woman is tied to the railroad tracks while, at the same time, a train is rushing toward her, and, also at the same time (and in another part of the country), the hero is trying to alert a sleepy station master to the impending disaster. In actuality, each of these events occurs and is photographed separately, their dramatic relationship being established in the director's study and in the film editor's workroom. In this sense, the film as an art form is quite similar to music; time, in the former, and tempo, in the latter, are artificially created, an illusion of eye or ear produced through technical means, just as the painter produces the illusion of depth on a two-dimensional canvas. In another sense, however, the film is like the novel, since the director and the novelist are both limited largely to the past tense. The movie viewer (or reader) is always aware that what he is seeing (or reading) has already happened, that it is a record and reproduction of events rather than the events themselves. Even in "present tense" novels, such as William Faulkner's *As I Lay Dying,* the reader is continually aware of the "pastness" of the events unfolded before him.

Television is different. It introduces an element into literature that cannot be as convincingly expressed in novels or films, namely, real time. On live television the presentation of the action and its perception by the audience are virtually simultaneous. There is no film to be developed, and there are no words to be printed. If we add to this the fact that the aesthetic distance between performer and audience closely approximates the "real" distance that separates people when they are conversing, we may understand why on television the sense of the actual is greater than in any other medium. To put it another way, the grammar of television communicates largely in the "present tense," and, as a consequence, television achieves its most compelling effects when it reveals the illusion of the "thing itself" happening in the here and now.

We have implied earlier that this sense of the actual has been exploited with success by such television dramatists as Paddy Chayefsky. But television plays, even when they are "live," still have the element of "pastness," since the audience can confidently assume that the author, director, and actors have carefully planned each word and action in advance. There are, however, other kinds of television "dramas"—we have called them "actuality narratives"—in which the sense of the actual is not only veritable but essential. Without it the presentations would be pointless. For example, *This Is Your Life,* for all of its artificialities, probably owes as much of its longevity to the inherent drama in an unpredictable situation as it does to its public exposure of what are essentially private matters. Certainly, the campaign debates of the presidential candidates drew much of their excitement from their sense of the actual and unpredictable.

This aesthetic dimension of television was recognized by the drama critic, Walter Kerr, who coined the term *visual essay* to describe programs which draw their main source of appeal from the sense of actuality and immediacy conveyed by television. The term subsumes such diverse programs as Leonard Bernstein's "demonstration-lectures," Mike Wallace's interviews, and the President's press conferences.

It is important to note that these programs have in common not only their sense of immediacy and actuality but (to continue the grammatical analogy) a sense of the "first person"; that is, there is direct, informal, and intimate communication with the audience. This mixture of intimacy and actuality probably accounts for the magnetism of the *Jack Paar Show*, which, despite its frequent commercial interruptions, communicates with a directness and candor that is possible only on television. No doubt the mixture plays a part in the appeal of Dave Garroway's *Today* show, as well as in the effectiveness of the sprightly Huntley and Brinkley commentaries.

> Over television, quietly and informally, great men of the age have talked to us. A Robert Frost or Frank Lloyd Wright tells about his life and work. There is astonishing intimacy. Throughout the great man's life, few human beings have looked on his face so long and closely as does the television viewer during such a program. Here intimacy and simplicity help give narration the most dramatic impact it can achieve.
>
> Erik Barnouw
> *Mass Communication*

This mixture has also been used with notable success for journalistic purposes. For example, probably one of the most dramatic visual essays ever presented on television was the "Army-McCarthy" hearings, in which the television camera, as incisively as any characterization written by Herodotus or Carlyle, penetrated to the essential qualities of public figures. The presentation of the national political conventions has also been a visual essay in which, on one network, Huntley and Brinkley, in the roles of a modern-day Addison and Steele, went beyond the observable events to make deep although humorous comments on American culture.

Whatever they are called—visual essays, actuality narratives, or something else—it would appear that television's most natural and compelling resource is its ability to communicate ideas and reveal events and people with a sense of intimacy and truthfulness. Perhaps the single most important characteristic shared by such television "personalities" as Arthur Godfrey, Jack Paar, Dave Garroway, Chet Huntley, David Brinkley, Edward R. Murrow, Eric Sevareid, Garry Moore, Arlene Frances and Mike Wallace is that they are not typical "show business" people. Neither do they appear to be actors, in a theatrical sense. They "play" themselves, and when their performances approach the histrionic, as occasionally in the case of Leonard Bernstein, there is a corresponding loss in effectiveness for many viewers. Another way of saying this is that on television, the untheatrical frequently tends to be more believable and more dramatic than the theatrical. This is an aesthetic principle which candidates for office ignore at their peril.

COMEDY

No body of literature is quite complete unless humor is amply and artfully represented. Television clearly satisfies this requirement, although its humor may more precisely be referred to as comedy since *comedy* connotes performances whereas *humor* suggests the written word. Aristophanes, for example, wrote comedies; Mark Twain's stories are humorous.

Television comedy has come, and continues to come, in various forms. Indeed, its range of comic forms is so wide that attempts at classification tend to be at an exceedingly high level of abstraction. One might, for example, distinguish between those comedians who essentially play themselves (Bob Hope) and those comedians who portray characters (Red

Skelton or Jackie Gleason). Or, one might distinguish between comedians who perform routines, that is, tell jokes,
do imitations, and fall on their faces (whether as "characters"
or not), and those who act in what are known as "situation
comedies."

Because such classifications tend to be vague, the discussion that follows is focused not on comic forms but on
selected comedians whose performances have lent distinction
to television or, perhaps what is quite as important in any
analysis of the medium, whose popularity reflects something
of our national character.

One must, therefore, begin with Milton Berle. For eight
years—from 1948 to 1956—Berle egotistically but quite
properly referred to himself as "Mr. Television." In five of
those years his *Texaco Star Theater* was the most popular
show on the air, and it was he, more than any other, who
made television itself a source of constant conversation in its
early years. In part, his success may be traced to the fact that
during much of his reign as "King of Television" there were
few serious pretenders to the throne. But the sources of his
popularity go deeper than the mere absence of competition,
as suggested by Gilbert Seldes' characterization of Berle as
"the triumph of the hotfoot." Indeed, Berle's comedy often
was at about the level of fun that people of unsophisticated
sensibilities enjoy when witnessing a well-executed "hotfoot."
His milieu was "low" comedy, which he brought to television
directly from New York night clubs but which had been a
staple in vaudeville. The image he projected was that of a
loud, physical, and incipiently vulgar egotist who seemed more
amused at his own jokes than anyone else was. For years a
substantial segment of the television audience cultivated a
curious fondness for this professional "life of the party," ad-
miring, perhaps envying, the abandon with which he "up-
staged" his betters and overwhelmed his equals. Possibly it was
precisely because the audience believed that Berle was in

reality the image he projected on the television screen that they remained fascinated by him for so long. There are few things more destructive to good comedy than manufactured brashness. Berle was genuinely brash, a fact that was unmistakably communicated by the television camera.

The reasons for Berle's decline on the *Texaco Star Theater* are directly related to the reasons for his ascent. The very brashness for which he was noted became too familiar, and because his comedy was uninstructive, it bred at least mild contempt. Also, weekly exposure is a phenomenon to which the television comedian is especially vulnerable. Berle learned, as did Jerry Lewis later, that television performers whose comedy is not about anything except themselves can sustain their popularity only so long as they retain the audience's affection. When affection leaves, obscurity is not far behind.

Whereas Berle was the first to bring the routines and palaver of the night-club floor to television, Sid Caesar was the first to bring to the medium the more substantial arts of satire and parody. He also brought with him, unlike Berle, a company of comedians admirably suited to assist him. From 1949 to 1954, Imogene Coca, Carl Reiner, and Howard Morris, among others, joined the multitalented Caesar in lampooning almost everything from modern art and Japanese films to quiz shows and westerns. Television, in particular, provided *Your Show of Shows* with its richest source of ridicule and, at one time or another, Caesar and his group satirized almost every one of television's literary "genres." The essential quality in Caesar's comedy was that, like Chaplin, most of his skits made a social comment. As a consequence, for all of its physicalness, often approaching slapstick, Caesar's comedy was invariably edifying. The audience was continually aware that it was observing not merely a funny man but a performer making fun of man and doing it at the expense of subjects that are not always looked upon as sources of humor. Although Caesar has not made regular appearances on television since 1958, the satiric tradition he began was carried on most successfully by the recently dissolved Steve Allen troupe. Not nearly so consistently "serious" as Caesar's *Your Show of Shows,* the *Steve Allen Show* treated with comic irreverence such subjects as military organizations, Princess Margaret's marriage, and—in the sturdiest tradition of satire—the hand that fed it, the commercial message.

In American culture, marriage is generally regarded as a natural source of comedy, and it was to this subject that Jackie Gleason turned with success after an inauspicious beginning on television. Although his character, Ralph Kramden, was the main focus of *The Honeymooners,* Gleason, like Caesar, enlisted the help of other comedians, each of whom was as capable as he. Gleason, Audrey Meadows, Art Carney, and Joyce Randolph played the roles of the Kramdens and Nortons, two improbable but likeable couples who carried on the battle of the sexes in a more full-bodied manner than Thurber's line-drawn characters. Unlike Thurber's men, Kramden, the bus driver, and Norton, the sewer digger, were always and clearly the inferiors of their respective mates. Whereas the wives appeared to be eminently sensible, if not always refined, the husbands were consistently boorish and repeatedly fumbled their way to absurd resolutions of simple and sometimes unnecessary problems. This pattern of the sensible wife and ineffective husband recurs frequently on television "situation comedy." One finds this pattern, for example, in *The Life of Riley, The Adventures of Ozzie and Harriet,* and *The Danny Thomas Show.*

Perhaps the most notable exception to this rule of situation comedy was the *I Love Lucy* show, where the wife, not the husband, appeared consistently clownish. Beginning in 1951 and competently supported by Desi Arnaz, William Frawley, and Vivian Vance, Lucille Ball romped through eight years of television's zaniest comedy. Probably the most gifted comedienne television has produced, Lucy was most successful at slapstick. Irrepressible, unsubtle, loud, and yet eccentrically intelligent, her appeal was largely to the audience's sense of the absurd. Like the Marx brothers, she represented the nihilistic impulse that dwells beneath the surface in many of us. But whereas Groucho's denial of all conventional standards sprang from a seeming amorality, Lucy's denial of logical standards invariably grew out of good intentions.

Many people feel that television comedy is the poorer for her absence, as it is for the absence of Gleason, Caesar, and Allen. But television is perhaps the only medium in which comedy is given a central place.

Because of this emphasis, we may be assured that exciting comedians will be continually exposed to the public. For example, our newest group of social satirists—sometimes called "sit-down comics"—has found in television an eager outlet for its seriocomic assaults on American values. Mort Sahl, Shelley Berman, Bob Newhart, and Mike Nichols and Elaine May were all catapulted to fame as a result of frequent, although not regular, appearances on television. Their quiet monologues (or, in the case of Nichols and May, dialogues) present an interesting contrast to the more frenetic performances of the Berle-Silvers-Skelton-Gleason type of comedian. However, the new comics are confronted by two obstacles not faced by many of their predecessors. First, the wide base of television's audience—at once a challenge and frustration to all television artists—might require some of these comedians to dilute the pungency of their routines, or even worse, compromise their points of view. Social criticism, in general, and satire, in particular, are not received with equal enthusiasm by all the segments of television's vast audience. Second, the format used by these comedians seems less suited to regular television appearances than the "situation comedy." The monologist requires a new set of jokes for each of his appearances on television, a requirement that would seem exceedingly difficult to fulfill in a thirty-nine week series.

MISCELLANEOUS PROGRAMS

The types of programs discussed above are by no means all of those in which the English teacher might have a professional interest. Several others are worth mentioning here.

Because the scope of the English curriculum is expanding, the teacher of English will be interested in such programs as *Twentieth Century, CBS Reports, Expedition!, Close-Up!,* and *Project 20.* These programs, as well as interview shows, such as *Meet the Press* and *Face the Nation,* are educational not only because they present ideas but also because they provide the audience with an opportunity to increase its understanding of the language of political, social, and economic discourse.

Children's programs would also be of more than passing concern to teachers not only in terms of the kind of information they present but also in terms of the way the information is presented. One of the best children's programs on television is *Captain Kangaroo,* which is notable for the unfailing respect it shows for the intelligence of its young viewers. Unlike the hosts on many children's programs and teachers in many classrooms, the Captain does not patronize the children by his tone, manner, or vocabulary. *Huckleberry Hound,* Don Herbert's *Mr. Wizard,* the *Shirley Temple Show* and the *Shari Lewis Show* are other children's programs of high merit.

Although the use of feature films on television does nothing to further the continued exploration of television's unique qualities as a communication form, the practice, nevertheless, affords the audience an opportunity to see many films of distinction, some of which are no longer shown in movie theaters. *Silents Please! The Late Show* (and its siblings, *The Early Show* and *The Late, Late Show*), and similar programs have shown such movies as *The Jazz Singer, The Shiek, High Noon, Odd Man Out, The Treasure of Sierra Madre, The Informer,* and *The Good Earth.* Thus, in spite of the fact that these films are interrupted for commercials, television allows the teacher and his students to study still another art form.

Our purpose in this chapter, as stated earlier, has been to demonstrate that television possesses a "literature" of its own, one which deserves to be given serious consideration. Of course, millions of school children already give it such consideration. However, teachers of English must help the children qualify their enthusiasm with thoughtful criticism.

PART TWO

The Classroom Study of Television

The purpose of Part Two of this book is to suggest to the teacher specific procedures that will give direction and force to the study of television in the classroom. Many of these procedures will be neither novel nor mysterious to teachers of English. In the first place, some of the attitudes and methods commonly employed in the teaching of literature are equally applicable to the study and teaching of television. For example, teachers as a rule require their students to think systematically about a novel, a short story, or a poem. Similarly, teachers will be urged—as a kind of first principle— to encourage their students to think systematically about television programs. In the second place, many teachers have already given some consideration to the problem of teaching television and possibly have evolved procedures not unlike those to be suggested here. The suggestions made below are, in fact, based on the experiences of teachers from all over the country who have been engaged, in one way or another, in the study of television.

In consideration of the wide variety in the training of teachers, in the degrees of flexibility of the English curriculum, in types of students, and in teaching situations, we have arranged the suggestions in a kind of spectrum, beginning with the simplest and proceeding to increasingly complex activities. Thus, a teacher may select those suggestions which seem most appropriate to his particular situation.

Announcement on Bulletin Board

An announcement of an important program tacked on a bulletin board is probably the simplest way to introduce television to the classroom. Such a procedure has at least two important advantages. The first and most obvious is that it alerts students to programs of merit—perhaps a play by Shakespeare or Ibsen, or an adaptation of a Robert Louis Stevenson or an A. A. Milne story. The second and more important is that it represents the beginning of a critical appraisal of television. In the very process of selecting a program and encouraging students to watch it, the teacher is functioning as a critic, making judgments of a kind that ultimately students will have to make. Of course, the teacher can play it safe by posting only announcements of adaptations of "classics." But he may also wish to recommend programs of a more contemporary nature which in his judgment will be worth watching.

However, teachers need to recognize that if the announcement is allowed to stagnate on the bulletin board, student interest is likely to stagnate as well. The announcement, therefore, should be changed regularly, generally at least once a week.

Announcement
Made in Class

An announcement made by the teacher of a forthcoming television program provides an additional dimension of academic approval that is not provided by a posted announcement. Even though no discussion follows, the teacher's words will lend a sense of urgency to the suggestion and may help to focus student interest. Particularly in the elementary grades, if a teacher does nothing more than announce that, say, *Peter Pan* is being televised on a Thursday evening, he has done much to raise the sights of his students to the opportunities television offers. The result may be that on Thursday evening, many parents might be surprised to observe their child reject his usual program in favor of James M. Barrie.

Of course, the teacher need not feel that his recommendations should be limited to plays alone. Programs like *Meet the Press, Face the Nation,* or *Issues and Answers,* for example, will afford youngsters the opportunity to observe how the various arts of language are used either to sharpen arguments or to expose the arguments oɪ others. Programs like *Captain Kangaroo* and *Mr. Wizard* will help younger children widen their range of interests and in so doing will increase their linguistic sophistication. The uses of language, in whatever context, are inevitably the concern of the teacher of English, and it follows that some consideration of news programs, documentaries, political discussions, and science programs falls within the scope of the English or language arts curriculum.

Display on Bulletin Board

If a television production is particularly important, then a special display on the bulletin board, prepared a few weeks in advance, will undoubtedly awaken interest. One teacher, reading the announcement of Maurice Evans' television production of *The Tempest*, prepared an attractive montage of drawings, photographs, and illustrative lines taken from the text. Since major productions generally are announced well in advance, teachers can write to local stations or sponsors to obtain printed material which will enliven the bulletin board and attract instant attention. Teachers can also make use of displays that appear in national magazines or in featured articles in *Studies in the Mass Media*, published by the National Council of Teachers of English.

Student Television Committee

The three suggestions made above are, of course, elementary ways of introducing television to the classroom and cannot be expected to do much more than focus student attention on some significant programs. Organizing a student television committee is, similarly, a minimal procedure for directing student attention to quality television. But the procedure differs from the others in that the responsibility for keeping abreast of current television offerings is with the student rather than the teacher. This is obviously no minor matter since successful teaching can scarcely begin until students assume the responsibility to participate actively in the learning process.

Students, therefore, should be entrusted to keep the bulletin board, write announcements on the blackboard, and make oral announcements in class. The teacher at first may have to instruct students in ways of obtaining reliable information concerning programs, but ultimately students ought to be able to proceed on their own initiative. The teacher might also wish to help the committee in its preparation of a bulletin board. A bulletin board, aside from its value as a method of commanding attention, provides students with an opportunity to express a wide range of interests and talents. For example, a Leonard Bernstein program on jazz may lead students to display on the bulletin board an essay on the origins of jazz, photographs of jazz musicians, a sketch of Bernstein himself, album covers, and two or three book jackets of important works on jazz. Such a bulletin board would require students to consult with the librarian in their search for appropriate materials. Both the librarian and the teacher will find that they can help students to sharpen their interests and discipline their talents if the bulletin board is taken seriously and high standards are demanded of the student's work. Teachers who have made use of the Student Television Committee have found that unless the committee is given careful guidance, interest flags and the project becomes perfunctory. Some teachers, moreover, appoint a new committee each week, thus involving every student in the undertaking.

Special Class Assignment

Not infrequently during the course of a semester, a television program of compelling interest will cry out for something more than mere notice in the classroom. Although the teacher may find it inconvenient or even unnecessary to pause for a week's time to deal with such a program, he may wish to spend at least a day or possibly two teaching about it. Accordingly and with admirable flexibility, he may announce to his students that their assignment to read a short story or to write a composition has been changed to the viewing of a special television production.

One important injunction must be interjected here. Teachers who have tried this procedure have found that they cannot insist on everyone's viewing the same program, or, for that matter, any television program at all. Although most students have access to a television set, some may not be free to watch at the time the program is being presented. As noted in Part One, television viewing, unlike reading, tends to be a family activity, and a parent who is prepared to see and hear Lawrence Welk may not accept the Sacco-Vanzetti story as an adequate substitute. In other words, teachers must remember that television is so much a part of the warp and woof of the evening hours that a seemingly innocent assignment may tear the fabric of family peace. Where such a problem can be anticipated, the teacher might have his students engage in "team watching," that is, suggest that a group of students assemble at the home of one to watch the program together. For those students who will be unable to watch the program, the teacher should provide a substitute assignment. If possible, this assignment should be in a related area. The reading of a short story, a one-act play, or an essay may then offer a basis for comparison with a television production.

The "special" assignment does not require extensive preparation and generally results in an informal lesson in which students discuss their reactions as naturally as they would a book, a movie, or a play. Such informality is not to be derogated, for it puts a television program into the same category as these art forms, where, intrinsically, it belongs. On the other hand, informality in an academic context sometimes encourages dilletantism, or worse, carelessness. The teacher must guard against these attitudes toward television, just as he guards against them toward other literary forms. He may wish, therefore, to structure his students' comments in a way that will maintain informality and at the same time cultivate the habit of disciplined analysis. For example, if the television program is a play, say, Robert Alan Aurthur's *The Sound of Different Drummers,* the teacher might ask his students to discuss the plot, the theme, and the characterization, much as if the students had organized a theater party, gone to see a stage play, and returned to school the next day to review their impressions. This does not mean that the teacher must cover all these details in academic fashion. With a class of "slow" students, the teacher might be content to go over the plot and then allow his students to discuss actions or dialogue that they did not understand. For an "advanced" class, a more sophisticated approach might be used. The teacher, whose homework always exceeds in depth and volume that required of his students, might locate the passage in Thoreau from which "the sound of different drummers" was borrowed. After reading the excerpt to his students, he may invite them to compare Thoreau's meaning with Robert Alan Aurthur's. Or, he may briefly recount for his students the cultural conditions which inspired Thoreau to nonconformity and ask his students to identify those conditions in our present environment which might have led Aurthur to construct such a play.

If the television program is a documentary, say, *CBS Reports' Who Speaks for the South?* the teacher might direct his students' remarks to the question of the program's "point of view." He might ask them to discuss, for example, which people they sympathized with and which ones they disliked. And, more pertinently, he might try to have his students articulate the reasons for their feelings. Although this program tried to present different sides of a controversial question fairly, it is important for students to realize that the movie or television camera injects a point of view by the very process of selecting one thing for emphasis and another for neglect.

In fact, any documentary of this kind, *Cast the First Stone, The Population Explosion,* or *The Jazz Age,* will very likely motivate the teacher to engage his students in a discussion of "objectivity" in reporting. Since perception itself is a process of selection (no one can see "all" of any event), the teacher might invite his students to formulate an operational definition of objective reporting and then discuss with them the ways in which various reporters on television attempt to achieve objectivity.

The teacher must remember that he cannot expect to do too much when giving a special class assignment. Since he is allowing only one or two days for discussion, he must accept the fact that his lesson will be superficial. And yet superficiality has certain virtues. In this instance, the teacher is demonstrating to his students, even if in a brief and broad effort, that the content of television can be as relevant to the classroom as many things from books or the stage. The sources of maturing experiences are not the monopoly of a few forms of communication, and the teacher is giving notice, so to speak, that television programs need to be and can be thoughtfully evaluated.

As a result of a special class assignment, the students may

find themselves asking searching questions of television programs they were not assigned to watch. A student who has never thought of it before may quite unexpectedly wonder why Beaver in *Leave It to Beaver* manages to solve problems that confound the other members of the family, or why Matt Dillon of *Gunsmoke* does not marry Kitty, or why Jim Anderson of *Father Knows Best,* unlike almost everyone else, does not have financial problems. Actually, these are rather sophisticated questions and experienced teachers will not expect them to arise quickly and readily. Nevertheless, the special class assignment has the virtue of relating the serious business of evaluating literature to the seemingly passive business of watching television.

In addition to representing a first step toward a serious consideration of television in the classroom, the special class assignment can be useful as an aid in teaching about things other than television. Although we are primarily concerned in this book with the value of television as a unique form of communication worthy of study in itself, it would be short-sighted not to mention its value as a carrier of information and ideas about subjects normally included in the English curriculum. For example, teachers and students who in 1960 were studying the structure of the English language might with great profit have turned to television when Bell Telephone presented *The Alphabet Conspiracy.* This program, which has been shown several times and which stars Dr. Frank Baxter and the talented Hans Conreid, is concerned with the science of language and explains in popularized fashion the basic assumptions, methodology, and terminology of linguistics. Don Herbert's *Mr. Wizard,* on one occasion, also dealt with the science of language. And, of course, Bergen Evans' *The Last Word* was concerned each week with problems of usage and grammar. If the teacher is willing to make use of such programs, he may ask his students to view one of them in lieu of or as a supplement to their regular assignment.

Then, too, teachers should not overlook the fact that television is in itself a constant and interesting source of linguistic information. Teachers who wish to describe to their students the various dialects of English will find satisfying examples on television—the New England speech of President Kennedy or Henry Cabot Lodge, the Texan drawl of Vice President Johnson, the midwestern twang of comedian Herb Shriner. Courageous teachers might even wish to bring to their students' attention, for the purposes of analysis, the colorful vocabulary of Dizzy Dean or the quaint but obscure syntax of Casey Stengel. The point is that with the exception of face-to-face communication, television is probably the most abundant source of linguistic experience that students have. Whether a teacher is interested in prescribing a particular set of speech patterns or concerned with increasing his students' sensitivities to the fascinating varieties of American English, television can be a useful aid. To introduce a unit on the social and economic utility of standard English, one teacher required his students to view two programs, *Father Knows Best* and *The Life of Riley*. The students were asked to note the differences between the speech patterns of Jim Anderson (played by Robert Young) and Chester Riley (played by William Bendix) and, at the same time, observe corresponding differences in their professions, status, and dress. One student observed that Riley's language, although apparently adequate for his "blue-collar" job, would not take him very far as an insurance salesman (Anderson's profession). The same student also discovered that Riley's limited vocabulary frequently frustrated his attempts to communicate with members of a different social class, while Anderson appeared to function with equal effectiveness among all kinds of people.

Another teacher, in introducing a brief unit on "linguistic snobbery," assigned her students the task of identifying the dialects, especially the "foreign accents," that tend to be sources of humor or, under certain circumstances, ridicule.

Using television as one source of information, the students discovered, among other things, that the Spanish-English of Desi Arnaz or Bill Dana ("My nay . . . Jose Jimenez"), the Italian-English of Pat Harrington, Jr. (Guido Panzini), and the Yiddish-English of Mollie Goldberg appeared to be objects of humor in themselves. A third teacher hoping to make his students aware of the changing character of language and, at the same time, wishing to increase his students' vocabulary required the class to note any new words or forms heard on television. One student discovered that sports announcers commonly use "flied" as the past tense of "hit a fly" ("Mazeroski flied to right"). Another student, inevitably, recognized the increasing use of *like* as a conjunction. A third student discovered the use of *science* as a verb, and a fourth listed as words she had never heard before: *perambulate, cogitate, genuflect,* and *insipid.* The dialogue of the television western is yet another source of information about the English language, and one teacher led his students through a happy and informative investigation of the dialect—even if it is a literary one—of the cowboy.

Such uses of television as these may be incorporated in the special class assignment procedure, which is to say that the teacher may depart for a day or two from the typical instructional materials used in class and focus his students' attention on a particular television program.

Brief Unit Isolated from Regular Curriculum

Sometimes a teacher may wish to prepare the class for a special television program and accordingly will develop a brief unit which is isolated from the other elements in the curriculum. Of course, some productions require little preparation; in fact, too much preparation may blunt the fine edge of anticipation which sharpens our enjoyment of a literary experience. A preliminary discussion which reveals the ending of "The Ransom of Red Chief" before it actually appears on the television screen should win a special place for the teacher on Ko-Ko's list. In the case of Ibsen's *A Doll's House*, however, the students could profit from an introduction. A unit on *A Doll's House*, therefore, might be divided into three parts.

I. BEFORE THE TELECAST

The teacher may have the students read Ibsen's *A Doll's House* and lead them in a discussion of Ibsen as a social dramatist, the fight for women's rights, the present prejudice against women in many jobs. In the Europe of 1879, the right of women to participate in all the decisions of family life, let alone establish identities apart from the family, was a highly charged, debatable, and perhaps impertinent question. It is considerably more settled today, and our students, unless sufficiently prepared, might find many of Nora's fears and motivations quaint rather than moving. The teacher might help his students sharpen their sensitivities to the social context of the play by inviting them to consider the situation of "minority" groups today whose activities and opportunities are limited by social prejudices. In fact, one of the provocative points that might emerge from these discussions concerns the relative freedom of various literary media to explore controversial themes. The teacher can prepare a brief lecture to demonstrate that live social and political issues have frequently found a congenial home in the theater—from Aristophanes' *The Knights* to Lorraine Hansberry's *A Raisin in the Sun*. The teacher can then invite his students to identify themes that typically are not treated in such media as radio, the movies, or television because an exploration of them—in dramatic or other forms—might assail the prejudices or sensitivities of large numbers of people. In fairness, the teacher should also encourage students to think of and look for examples of television programs that transcend their audience's provincialism.

The purpose of such activities is to prepare the imagination of the students for the play, a preparation involving, among other things, the students' recognition of the theater as a form of social criticism.

II. DURING THE TELECAST

Although Ibsen was undoubtedly deeply interested in the social and psychological points of each of his "problem" plays, he was pre-eminently a dramatist; that is, he was at least equally concerned with the dramatic form in which he stated and explained the problem. Accordingly, the teacher might require his students while watching the play to formulate answers to questions regarding its structure and the structure of character development. For example, how do Nora's actions and words in the first act suggest the kind of person Ibsen intends her to be? At what point in the play does the audience become aware of Nora's need for individual identity? At what point in the play does Nora become aware of this need? What details are selected to portray Nora as an unequivocally sympathetic character?

Quite as important as these questions are those concerning the artistic resources of the television camera. For example, what role does the camera play in establishing Nora as the central character? In what instances does the camera reinforce (or perhaps render superfluous) certain dialogue? In what visual ways are Helmer's indignation, incredulity, and, finally, despair communicated?

In short, even in a brief unit of this kind, the teacher may help students to see that the content of a play and its form are inextricably related.

III. AFTER THE TELECAST

In addition to providing the students with an opportunity to discuss questions they were assigned to ask themselves during the telecast, the teacher will want to raise other important, albeit conventional, questions. For example, what is the play's significance for the modern audience? Is it dated? Are the characters two-dimensional, or do they possess the many-sidedness, even ambivalence, that characterizes most human behavior? However, the questions which require students to reflect on the play as a *television play* may contribute most to their grasp not only of the particular production they saw but also of certain characteristics of television itself. The students will need constant reminding that Ibsen wrote for the stage and that, as a consequence, not all of his dramatic devices are effective on television. The students might consider, for example, what dialogue or action was omitted from the television production. They might discuss whether or not these omissions added to or subtracted from the impact of the play. And they might speculate on the question of why the writer or director omitted or added certain material.

The teacher should not expect that the answers to these

questions will lead his students very far along the path toward an understanding of the nature of television. They will, of course, take his students a few steps and give direction to later and more penetrating studies. But the main purposes of this kind of unit are two: to give the students a prepared opportunity to see Ibsen, Shaw, Shakespeare, Dickens, Grimm, or Stevenson and to alert the students to some of the obvious differences between two literary forms.

One caution needs to be given. Television productions of classic plays or novels are often approached by their adapters as if the work had been written to be a "classic." In other words, television adaptations are often presented with a reverence that would have appalled the creators of the original works and offended their contemporary audiences. (The adapters, of course, are graduates of our own schools and have been taught, like most of their audience, to treat the classics preciously.) Therefore, the teacher might exercise care not to allow the aura of "greatness" surrounding these productions to stultify audience response. Unless our students can respond directly and with pleasure to their literary experiences, we will subvert our intentions to develop their interests any further. At the same time, the creators of television adaptations not infrequently alter the content and structure of the original for the purpose of gaining wider audience acceptance. This is a possibility to which the teacher will want to alert his students.

Brief Unit Within the Regular Curriculum

Some teachers will find that television can be included easily and effectively within a brief unit that is part of the curriculum. In this case, there is no need to shut the books in class and break the continuity of instruction. Probably the most fortuitous example of how classroom work can be combined with television is in the instance of a television adaptation presented at the same time that its original is being studied in class. Such coincidences are by no means rare, since there is no dearth of adaptations on television. But accidental simultaneity, while certainly possible, is much too restricting. The teacher, therefore, should create simultaneity by reversing the sequence; that is, by requiring his students to read a novel or short story or play that is scheduled to appear on television. In any given semester, three or four adaptations of stories the teacher would like his students to read anyway will appear on television. In the eighteen months prior to the spring of 1961, adaptations of the following works appeared on network television: *The Moon and Sixpence, Winterset, The Tempest, Arrowsmith, For Whom the Bell Tolls, The Killers, The Turn of the Screw, A Doll's House, Misalliance, What Makes Sammy Run?, The Devil and Daniel Webster, Ethan Frome, The Fallen Idol, Oliver Twist, Victory, Hamlet, The Human Comedy, Billy Budd, The Browning Version, Our Town, Old Man, Jane Eyre, Nana, Camille, Macbeth, The Three Musketeers, Lost Horizon, The Scarlet Pimpernel*, and *Winnie the Pooh*.

Whenever the teacher can arrange for his students to read the original of a television adaptation, he has an excellent opportunity to engage the class in a *cross-media analysis*. This term is used to describe the activity of comparing the content and form of a story presented in one medium with its content and form as presented in another. Obviously, adapting a story from one medium to another will involve changes. In analyzing the nature and extent of these changes, students can make considerable progress toward understanding the structure of literary form.

Teachers should not, however, make the mistake of assuming that an adaptation is necessarily and always the inferior of the original. In the first place, frequently such comparisons are analogous to the comparing of apples with oranges, which is to say that the adaptation may not be either better or worse, but different. Edwin Granberry's "A Trip to Czardis" is a sensitive, compassionate, and well-constructed short story. Robert Herridge's adaptation of it is a sensitive, compassionate, and well-constructed television play. The difference is not one of quality or integrity but of literary form. In the second place, adaptations are, in fact, sometimes better conceived and more movingly executed than their originals. Sophocles' *Oedipus Rex* was an adaptation of a Greek myth; Shakespeare's *Macbeth,* while not strictly an adaptation, had as its original source a story that appeared in Holinshed's *Chronicles;* and Stanley Kubrick's film *Paths of Glory* was a brilliant re-creation of an indifferent novel. In any case, the primary purpose of a cross-media analysis is not to discover which story is "better" (although such evaluations certainly should be made) but to discover something about the literary forms under investigation.

Cross-media analyses may be conducted in terms of specific questions within particular categories, as follows:

CHARACTER

1. How has the leading character been changed? For example, has he been made more likeable, handsomer, younger, wealthier, more forceful, more unequivocal?

2. Have minor characters been eliminated, added, or substantially altered?
3. Have relationships between characters been changed? For example, has a mistress in a book or play become a "friend" in the television adaptation?
4. Have other identifying characteristics been altered? For example, have specific religious, ethnic, or political affiliations been eliminated? Has a Communist become simply a "radical"?

SETTING

1. Has the place of the events been changed? Has Cuba become "a small Latin-American country"? Has Mississippi become "somewhere in the South"?
2. Have the settings been made more luxurious or more poverty stricken?
3. Have scenes been added or omitted?

LANGUAGE

1. Has profanity or obscenity been removed?
2. Have simpler or more explicit explanations been used?
3. Has dialogue been transferred from one character to another?
4. Has a descriptive passage been transformed into dialogue?

CONFLICTS

1. Has a single goal been substituted for the complex ends sought in the original?
2. Have complex motivations and solutions been reduced to single lines of action?

THEME

1. Have the philosophic or ideological bases for the action been removed? For example, has a man's political passion been replaced with a romantic one?
2. Has the original theme been eliminated or altered?
3. Has the theme been made more explicit?

STRUCTURE

1. Have incidents been added or omitted?
2. Have action sequences been expanded or compressed?
3. Has a descriptive passage been transformed into visual images?
4. Have symbolic images been visually communicated?

ETHICAL AND MORAL STANDARDS

1. Has virtue been made to triumph and sin been punished?
2. Have transgressions against contemporary values been rectified?

Several observations must be made about this list of questions. First, most of the questions stated here imply their converse; that is, if we ask if the adaptation removed the philosophic basis of the action, we must be equally prepared to ask if it supplied one that was absent from the original. Second, the categories and questions above are by no means exhaustive, and teachers might wish to add their own. At the same time, no teacher will wish to have his students attempt to answer as many questions as are listed above. The teacher will need to be selective, as always, in posing questions for his students to answer. Third, and most important, none of these questions is significant in itself. Each is worth asking only if the question, once answered, is followed by another, namely, "Why?" Students must do more than establish that a single goal was substituted for complex ones in the television adaptation of *For Whom the Bell Tolls* or that several characters were added in the adaptation of Faulkner's "Old Man." They must also consider why these changes were made, for in establishing the reasons for the changes, the students may obtain some clear glimpses of television's resources and limitations, as well as the resources and limitations of the medium with which television is being compared. In order to elaborate on this point, let us examine two examples of television productions that were adapted from highly successful short stories.

"THE KILLERS"

In Ernest Hemingway's short story, "The Killers," the intended victim, Ole Andreson, is directly involved in only one brief scene—when Nick Adams goes to Andreson's room to inform him of impending danger. The reader does not learn why Andreson is to be killed (Andreson says simply, "I got in wrong"), is not told what Andreson looks like (except that from his face one would not guess that he had once been a prize fighter), and is given only a few terse lines of dialogue as clues to what Andreson is feeling.

In A. E. Hotchner's television adaptation of "The Killers," much of this is changed. Andreson is not only shown in several scenes and provided with considerable dialogue but turns out to be none other than attractive Ingemar Johansson, who at the time happened to be the heavyweight champion of the world. Andreson is given ample opportunity to explain why his future is uncertain. The explanation makes Andreson's threatened extinction seem doubly unjust since the audience learns that his "crime" was born of a basic sense of decency: he honestly fought and won a fight he had promised to lose. The audience is also given a full opportunity to enter into Andreson's thoughts and thus to commiserate with his problem.

Other differences between the original and the adaptation are also apparent. For example, Hemingway refers to Sam, the Negro cook, as a "nigger" and depicts him as a great deal more cowardly than Nick and George, both white men. In Hotchner's version, the derogatory term is eliminated, and the Negro is depicted as only slightly more cautious than George and certainly not abject. Also, in the short story, Nick Adams, after warning Andreson, decides it is best for him to leave town. On television, Nick warns Andreson, goes to the police (who do not believe his story), and then arms himself with a rifle with which he hopes to defend Andreson.

At least a dozen other changes could be noted between the two versions, but let us consider some of the possible reasons for a few of the changes mentioned above. Why, for example, are Ole Andreson's and Nick Adams' parts in the television play expanded far beyond their parts in the short story. An obvious answer suggests itself immediately when one realizes that Hotchner was writing a play that had to run for approximately seventy-five minutes. (The entire program was "live" and ninety minutes long.) Yet Hemingway's "The Killers" is, after all, a brief short story, a form which by definition calls for economy. The form Hemingway employed did not require him to do more than suggest in minimum detail what his characters were like and, in particular, what motivated them. Hemingway allows the reader's imagination to supply the full particulars of the story.

Hotchner was working in a form which demands greater explicitness. A visual image is frequently more concrete and therefore more explicit than a verbal description. This does not necessarily mean that a visual image "tells more" than a verbal one. A visual image does, however, tell different and sometimes contradictory things. In this drama, Andreson's face, recognizable as that of a world's champion, clearly stamps the character as a successful fighter, not an indifferent one as the rest of the story suggests. Also, seventy-five minutes allows for greater specification of narrative detail, in fact, demands it.

Hotchner was required, accordingly, to make his story more narrative than philosophic. Hemingway's story is essentially one of ideas; Hotchner's version stresses action. Hemingway is chiefly concerned with the impact of one event on three people—and their symbolically different responses; Hotchner is chiefly concerned with Nick Adams' attempts to prevent the killing. Hemingway's Nick Adams is shocked by George's almost casual acceptance of life and is rendered passive by Andreson's resignation to his fate. Hotchner's

Adams is almost frenetically active, activity being better suited to a visual medium than passivity, and he ultimately revives Andreson's will to survive (perhaps a concession to an audience accustomed to "happy endings"). This ending, of course, drastically transforms the theme of the story. Hemingway seems to say that there are some things that can be neither fully understood nor changed, that must be accepted for what they are. Hotchner suggests almost the opposite, that no situation is beyond our understanding or improving if we are willing to expend a maximum effort.

Also, Hotchner uses the "flashback" as a means of revealing the events leading up to the decision to kill Andreson. In other words, in "present time" dramatic form, he discloses events preceding the basic story. Even if Hemingway had wished to inform his readers of how Andreson "got in wrong," it would have been difficult to do so within the form of his short story. Hemingway certainly would have had to sacrifice the rhythm of his story, for which he is justly renowned, for the sake of such detail. With more time at his disposal and using the standard techniques for signaling past events (the picture fades out and a new one fades in), Hotchner was able to supply the pertinent details of Andreson's ambiguous past.

We observed, also, that the character of Sam, the cook, was changed in the adaptation. The key question, again, is "Why?" Here we must keep in mind some characteristic differences between publishing and broadcasting, and, in particular, the greater artistic freedom that the former offers. That Hemingway's story first appeared in *Scribner's Magazine* in March, 1927, means, among other things, that it was read by a relatively small and probably homogeneous audience. Very likely there were few Negroes in the magazine's audience, and if there were many, that fact might not have made any difference to either Hemingway or *Scribner's*. Then, too, it must be remembered that in 1927 audiences were not so sensitive to stereotyping or so repulsed by its effects as they are in our own times. In any case, the writer of short stories or novels is certainly freer to depict members of minority groups in any way he wishes than is the television writer. The television writer, in consideration of the heterogeneity of his "mass" audience, must be more cautious in dealing with ethnic stereotypes. One may concede at once that in referring to Sam as a "nigger" the killers are quite in character, as is George in making the same reference. Understandably, however, Hotchner omitted the term, giving social discretion priority over artistic integrity. At the same time, Hotchner took the opportunity that an expanded form afforded to make of Sam something more than the literary stereotype of the "frightened Negro."

Finally, we might briefly consider the question of why the world's heavyweight champion was selected to play the role of Andreson. Of course, the name of the character suggests that he is of Swedish background (although nothing in Hemingway's dialogue suggests that he speaks with a Swedish accent). Also, Johansson appears to have sufficient intelligence to play the role with at least a modicum of skill. But probably overriding these considerations is the fact that Johansson is a celebrity. Celebrities attract large audiences, and large audiences are of more than passing concern to broadcasters, producers, and sponsors.

Having evolved from religious symbols, rituals, and proscriptions, the theater of ancient Greece was presided over by Dionysus—originally the god of fertility. Similarly, it may be said that the dramatic art of television is presided over by Hermes, god of commerce.

"A TRIP TO CZARDIS"

Edwin Granberry's short story, "A Trip to Czardis," originally appeared in *Forum* magazine in April, 1932. It tells of the final journey of two young boys to their father's prison cell immediately before the father is to be executed. During most of the story, the sons are unaware of their father's (and their own) plight, and not until the boys and their mother are returning home does the older son, Jim, realize he will never see his father again. Like "The Killers," "A Trip to Czardis" is highly condensed and subdued in tone; its elements are unfolded with reticence and, for the most part, by implication. The reader is never told what crime the father has committed, why it was committed or where. These facts, as in "The Killers," are irrelevant to the point of the story and are left to the reader's imagination to ponder. Also, the reader is never directly informed of the purpose of the boys' tragic trip to Czardis. Awareness of this purpose comes to the reader gradually and only by suggestion, never by direct statement.

Robert Herridge's adaptation of "A Trip to Czardis" took approximately twenty-six minutes to perform, which is to say that Herridge was not required, as Hotchner was, to expand substantially the parts of any of the characters or to alter the pace of the story. Herridge did contribute dialogue not found in the original, but mainly for the purpose of informing the audience of facts that Granberry reveals in narrative form. For example, in the short story, the reader is told that Daniel, the younger brother, has a "sickness against food." Herridge made this known solely through dialogue. Granberry also tells the reader that there are many wagons on the road to Czardis (suggesting, not actually saying, that they are carrying people who are curious to see the execution). Herridge, again, informed the audience of this only through dialogue. On the other hand, narratively, Granberry tells almost nothing about the mother, relying mostly on her grim and sparse language to communicate the singular strength with which she accepts the tragedy. To communicate this same fact, Herridge naturally relied heavily on his camera, which he persistently focused on the mother's face.

Perhaps the main difference between the original and the

adaptation is in the addition of a "flashback" scene in the latter. Jim has apparently been to Czardis once before, a visit that was both happy and memorable for him and his father. He has, in fact, so often repeated the details of the trip to his younger brother that Daniel begins to believe that he, himself, was there. In the short story, the reader learns of all this through a brief exchange between Jim and Daniel:

> "All the way we are goen this time. We won't stop at any places, but we will go all the way to Czardis to see Papa. I never see such a place as Czardis."
> "I recollect the water tower—"
> "Not in your own right, Dan'l. Hit's by my tellen it you see it in your mind."
> "And lemonade with ice in it I saw—"
> "That too I seen and told it to you."
> "Then I never seen it at all?"
> "Hit's me were there, Dan'l. I let you play like, but hit's me who went to Czardis. Yet I never till this day told half how much I see. There's sights I never told."

Herridge apparently felt that the form in which he was working would permit a more detailed development of Jim's previous trip without sacrificing the compactness of the story. Thus, as Jim and Daniel sat in the back of the wagon which carried them to Czardis, Daniel asked Jim to recount once again the details of his previous trip. Jim obliged his brother, and in "flashback" a brief scene was enacted between Jim and his father. The father bought Jim a cup of iced lemonade and pointed out the impressive water tower to him. The scene did not add any important new facts to the story, but the juxtaposition of a happy moment of the past with the misery of the present had the effect of making the present even more painful than it was.

Another important difference between the original and the adaptation is that in the latter, Herridge omitted some brief but important images included in the short story. As mentioned previously, Herridge did not show the other wagons that were journeying to Czardis. Neither did he show crowds of people walking toward the prison, nor a man sitting in the branch of a tree which overlooks the courtyard in which the father will be executed. These images are important in the short story, since they reveal the crowd's callous anticipation of the execution and thus make the family's isolation and sadness all the more poignant. Probably the best explanation for the absence of these visual images in the adaptation can be found in the limitations of television itself. The television camera, studio, and screen are not well suited to the projection of large groups or wide open spaces. More than five people on a set will involve constant regrouping and cutting in order to give the audience a clear view of faces. The farther the camera moves back, the less distinct are the faces and the less significant appears the crowd. Vastness is an illusion better achieved on a large movie screen. Within the confines of a television studio, it is even difficult to attempt. Herridge chose to "work in close," as is his custom, and no more than three people appeared on the screen at any one time. He limited the play almost entirely to scenes taking place indoors. Even the wagon which carried the family to and from Czardis was shot in "close-up" so that at no time could the audience see it in its entirety. In short, Herridge gave all of his attention to the faces of his main characters, alternately revealing little Daniel's bewilderment, Jim's growing maturity, the mother's disciplined misery.

Granberry concludes his story at the point where Jim realizes that he will never see his father again. Daniel does not know this yet, and on their return from Czardis, Daniel reminds Jim of the watch and chain their father gave them. The last line of the story is:

But Jim neither answered nor turned his eyes.

Herridge concluded his adaptation at the same point but allowed a guitar's lonely sounds and the camera's lens to "speak" the last line to the audience.

In spite of inevitable differences between these two versions, each literary form, in its way, is successful in communicating an almost unendurable sense of the tragic. In this case, the adapter, like the author of the original, is an artist who understands both the resources and limitations of his medium.

A final observation to be made about a cross-media analysis is that the teacher need not limit to two the number of media under investigation. In a brief unit (perhaps a week or slightly more) the teacher may not have time to guide his students through a comparative analysis of a story in, say, three different literary forms, but the teacher may consider the possibility in a more extensive unit. Certainly the opportunities are tempting when we face the almost contemporaneous appearance of a story in the form of a novel, stage play, film, and television play (as happened with *The Caine Mutiny*).

In addition to cross-media analyses, there are other ways of directing classroom attention to the television screen. If a novel is studied in class, the development of character becomes a subject for analysis. This analysis can be extended to television for comparison and contrast even when the novel and television program have only a tenuous connection with each other. If Beret in *Giants in the Earth* emerges as a real woman, whose gentle, guilt-ridden soul shrinks from the reality of the prairie, then she can be compared with a woman in a television play, perhaps a western, although it need not be one. The teacher might discuss with students how a novelist achieves a sense of wholeness in a character and compare these techniques with those of the television writer or director. The difference between a real character and a puppet can be demonstrated in both media, for television characters, even in westerns, are not necessarily two-dimensional.

Character analysis can give way to the study of endings as a clue to artistic integrity and literary worth. In the Greek theater when a god was lowered onto the stage in a mechanical device to help resolve with authority and justice an otherwise impossible situation, the playwright was admitting an artistic defeat, perpetrating a kind of literary fraud which has one modern counterpart in the last minute arrival of the United States Cavalry but which also has many other manifestations. The phrase, *deus ex machina,* "the god from the machine," has become standard in criticism and refers, of course, to awkward, unconvincing, or arbitrary means of resolving a plot. The teacher might require his students to read or view specific short stories, novels, films, and television plays and lead the class in a discussion of types of endings and what they reveal of their creators' attitudes toward their art and audience. The teacher might distinguish among the surprise ending (as in much of O. Henry and De Maupassant and in Rod Serling's *The Twilight Zone*), the contrived ending (as in Herman Wouk's novel, *The Caine Mutiny,* Shaw's *Heartbreak House,* and, of course, in many television westerns), and the "natural" ending in which the climax grows out of elements already in the story (as in Willa Cather's *Paul's Case,* Walter Van Tilburg Clark's *The Ox-Bow Incident,* Carol Reed's film, *Odd Man Out,* and Rod Serling's *Playhouse 90* production, *In the Presence of Mine Enemies*).

Units of this kind need not be sustained. If the process of analysis, comparison, and correlation seems unwieldy, the teacher can divide the class into committees, each responsible for one aspect of the subject. One committee can watch a television program to note the development of character; another, the types of conflict depicted; a third, the use of dialogue; a fourth, the types of endings; a fifth, the general themes. Or, the teacher might have one committee analyze character, conflict, dialogue, ending, and theme of a particular television program, while another committee analyzes the same elements in a short story, and still another committee, the same elements in a play or film. A final report or a panel discussion at the end of the week can bring the unit to a satisfactory close.

Extensive Unit

The extensive unit on television does not have to be correlated with items in the curriculum, for it becomes part of the curriculum itself. Instead of studying a novel or a group of plays or poems for several weeks, a class can undertake the study of television drama for its own sake and from various points of view. An ambitious project for a class would involve the study of television programs as an expression of American life, a study that would extract from television plays, comedies, musicals, and commercials the values that television seems to find inherent in American life. The men and women who create television programs share to a great extent the fears, hopes, ambitions, and conceits of their audiences. Thus, television programs tend to be an informative index of many of the operative, as well as theoretical, values in our society. Perhaps the family show would be a natural starting point for such a study, although almost any of television's genres could do just as well. The teacher might require his students to view two or three of several possible programs, such as *Father Knows Best, Bachelor Father, December Bride, The Real McCoys, Lassie, The Life of Riley, National Velvet, Leave It to Beaver.* Each student, or possibly each committee of students, might then be assigned a particular set of questions to answer. The following questions, for example, might obtain some provocative answers:

1. *In what ways are the various members of the family depicted?* Does the father smoke? Does he drink? Is he authoritarian? Is the mother more sensitive and refined than the father? What are the primary interests of the

children—school? sports? their social life? What are their ambitions?

2. *What is the economic status of the family?* Is the family prosperous? If so, what symbols of prosperity are in evidence? Does the family own a car? Does the family live in a house or an apartment? Is the family served by a maid or butler? Are there more than two or three children in the family? Does the family seem to be a "typical" one? Does the family live in the city, the country, the suburbs?

3. *What are the family's cultural identifications?* What is the family's religion? What are its politics? If these identifying characteristics are not revealed, why do you suppose they aren't? Does the family appear to be well educated? If so, what symbols of education or culture are in evidence? Are there books in the house? Are there paintings on the wall? Does the family characteristically use "standard" English? Do the children appear to spend as much time watching television as you do? Are most children as mischievous as Dennis the Menace? Are dogs as intelligent as Lassie appears to be?

4. *What kinds of problems confront the family?* Does the father have financial problems? Is there a concern for large social or political issues? Are there any conflicts that appear to be irreconcilable? How are problems solved—by chance? by thoughtful reasoning? Are the problems of these television families similar in kind and degree to the problems of your own family?

5. *What explicit values are preached?* Is the audience encouraged to "get along well with others"? Is it encouraged to be friendly at all costs? Is it encouraged to be tolerant? to be ambitious? to be patriotic? to be kind to animals? to be kind to parents?

The answers to these and other questions the teacher or students may formulate will say something about American family life as one television literary form interprets it. For example, if family shows typically do not reveal anything about the religious life of the families involved (and we suspect few do), what inferences can be drawn from this? Does this mean that Americans are not religious? Does it reflect a feeling that sectarian religious differences are not important? Does it reflect a view that one's religion is no one else's business, not even to be revealed in a dramatic context? Does it reflect a desire to avoid offending the beliefs of a large and heterogeneous audience?

Again, assuming that few such problems will be found, what tentative inferences may be drawn from the absence of financial problems in these plays? Does this suggest that most Americans do not have serious "money problems"? Or, does it suggest that money problems are so prevalent and real that Americans do not care to witness fictionalized and detailed accounts of them? This last question opens up the whole area of "escapism" in our television literature; that is, do family shows tend to be unreal? Do they show us the way we are? the way we should be? Or, do they depict a world which has only the appearance of reality but in which all problems are minor and all can be resolved?

Although some of the questions listed above are clearly rhetorical, others are just as clearly open to a variety of possible answers, and the teacher and his students would be wise to approach their inquiries unencumbered by preconceived notions.

Preconceived notions are also a burden in the investigation of television commercials. Although in Part One of this book we gave them little attention, commercials are, in fact, one of the sharpest indices of American values to be found on television. Commercials, perhaps more directly than any other form, communicate what their creators think their viewers believe is the "good life." Sometimes prepared with taste and imagination, commercials present to the careful and objective observer a more or less complete stock of cultural symbols,

symbols which carry in their form the prevailing standards of economic and social success. The teacher might wish, therefore, to follow up the study of family shows with an analysis of television commercials. He might have each of his students analyze two or three commercials in the following way:

1. Provide a description of each commercial, including its setting, its language, its music (if any), the type of persons depicted in it, and the kind of activity in which they are engaged.
2. Also, describe the product that is being advertised and the responses of the various persons in the commercial to the product.
3. Then answer the following questions:
   a. What needs or desires are appealed to—social acceptance? good health? independence? economic security? comfort? time-saving?
   b. Are there any implied consequences in one's failing to purchase the product? Will one lose dates? fail to get married? spend money, time, energy needlessly?
   c. To what extent do you think these needs are prevalent in American society? For example, do your parents and their friends (as well as you and your friends) desire social acceptance? comfort? luxury? To what extent do these needs influence their and your behavior?
   d. If actual people are employed to give testimonials, what does their status as celebrities tell us about American life? Who is Lew Burdette? Elsa Maxwell? Jack Paar? Buster Keaton? Why are these people used for testimonials? Why should we be expected to emulate them?
   e. Is the commercial harmonious with the content and tone of the program it serves? Is the commercial in good taste? Does the commercial appeal to the immaturity of a particular audience? Would this commercial be more or less acceptable if presented at a different time period?

This list of questions is not intended to be exhaustive, and each teacher will no doubt think of many other questions which, in their being answered, will yield insights into the values of our society. But answering questions such as these is certainly not all the teacher will want his students to do. A unit of this kind is scarcely complete until the students extend their inquiries beyond the television screen. Accordingly, the teacher might require his students to analyze best-selling books (*The Power of Positive Thinking, Only in America, Marjorie Morningstar*), hit plays (*The Dark at the Top of the Stairs, The Tenth Man*), and popular songs ("My Little Corner of the World," "Where the Boys Are"). The students might speculate, in the form of essays, on why such works are appealing and to what kinds of audiences. The teacher will help the students to discern patterns of meaning in these examples of popular culture if he reveals the fact that frequently such works are expressions of prevailing fantasies and immaturities, and that almost certainly they reflect cultural biases and preoccupations. Advanced students might be assigned to read books in which these biases and preoccupations are made explicit and are subject to analysis: David Riesman's *The Lonely Crowd*, William Whyte, Jr.'s, *The Organization Man*, C. Wright Mills' *The Power Elite*, Gilbert Seldes' *The Public Arts*, and Charles Wright's *Mass Communication*. These students might then share the content of these books with the class by presenting reports on them.

Since the main purpose of this unit is to help students "read" the cultural symbols that surround them, the teacher should feel free to explore various media of communication, not only television. This unit becomes, in a real sense, the study of American culture as it is revealed in our popular arts.

Another kind of extended unit involving a close, critical scrutiny of television could have as its aim the students' greater awareness of stereotyping. Stereotypes are, of course, used in all forms of literature and occasionally with good purpose and effect. In fact, language itself may be said to be a stereotype since all words with lexical content are abstractions; that is, they omit significant distinguishing details. But stereotyped thinking, as we know too well, can be dangerous and more times than not is destructive to literary effort. The teacher, therefore, might select one of television's popular genres for analysis and then lead his students in a discussion of the ways in which writers of, say, "cops and robbers" stories employ stock characters. Or, the teacher might approach the subject from the other way around. He might list different professions and assign students the task of determining to what extent these professions are stereotyped on television programs. Are teachers, for example, portrayed as being docile and absent-minded? Are scientists portrayed as eccentric, if not psychotic? Are athletes portrayed as illiterate and single-minded? If such stereotypes are identified, and particularly if the students find them congenial, the teacher might make an effort to introduce the students either in person or in literature to people who defy the generalizations made about them. Such people, needless to say, can be found in television literature as well as in novels, short stories, and the theater.

An attractive unit of a different kind can be built on the basis that the television play is but another form of dramatic literature that is constantly responsive to the influence of new audiences and new media. In a sense, this unit becomes a comparative anatomy of drama. The teacher can begin with the drama closest to the students, the television play, and work backward in time. Or, if he prefers, he may begin with an older form of drama to show how the playwright reacted to the forces that shaped both the form and content of his work.

Since the history of drama is in itself an encyclopedic subject, the teacher can limit the scope of the unit by concentrating on three forms of the drama that can be studied easily in the classroom—ancient Greek drama, Shakespearean

drama, and finally, modern drama, which might be represented by the stage play, the motion picture, and the television
play. In each case, a typical play can be studied, with recordings, films, filmstrips, visits to the museum and to television
studios, if that can be arranged, supplementing the work. In
each case, again, the nature of the audience, the physical
properties of the stage, the mores of the time, and the special
problems of the playwright can be studied for their effect on
dramatic technique, characterization, dialogue, plot, and
theme.

Sophocles' *Electra,* for example, played to such a huge
audience (probably about 17,000) that the acting undoubtedly had to be stylized. The actors wore not only masks for
designation of character but also high-soled boots which
helped to increase both their literal and literary stature. Also,
the actors—usually no more than three—had to speak in
broad sweeps of dialogue that could be heard and understood
by onlookers perched high in the amphitheater.

Unlike the Athenian audience, the Elizabethan audience
was witnessing a play that was not part of an elaborate religious service. The audience at the Globe Theater was, from
all accounts, inclined to be excitable, individualistic, noisy,
and quarrelsome; and their attention had to be caught and
held by means of strong emotional appeal, slapstick, and
suspense. The television audience cannot even be seen, let
alone heard. It can, however, turn the dial and thus end communication unless the play makes an instant impact.

Furthermore, the television audience is far more heterogeneous than any theater audience in history. Sophocles pro-
ceeded under the assumption that his audience was thoroughly
acquainted with the literary and religious tradition from which
the form and the content of his play were derived. The
Athenian audience of the 5th century B.C. not only knew
poetry in epic, lyric, and dramatic form but could also ap-
preciate any deftly inserted historical, literary, or political

allusions. Aristophanes, for example, frequently included in his plays parodies of contemporary writers and philosophers with whose work, we can assume, the audience was intimate. Shakespeare did not have audiences of comparable homogeneity. Therefore, he frequently had recourse to a Prologue in which he stated clearly what the play was going to be about. The television playwright is even less certain of his audience. Ours is—as we like to call it—a pluralistic society which probably means, among other things, that most of us are equally unfamiliar with our traditions. At the same time, we are a "modern" audience, more influenced by Darwin and Freud than we realize. All of these facts shape the kind of work our writers will do, just as the facts of a past age structured the kind of work its writers did. Lest teachers feel that a unit of this kind is simply too broad to handle in class, let us outline a few of the salient elements that would emerge from a consideration of the development of drama.

The reading of *Electra* would demonstrate how Sophocles had to observe the unities of time, space, and action—principles that were dictated by the nature of the stage. Greek plays were performed in an open-air theater. Usually the only setting on the stage was a wooden façade. Thus, dramatists were confined to stories which reasonably and convincingly could take place out of doors—typically in front of a house, palace, or temple. Interior scenes were practically impossible to present. The Greek dramatist also made use of a chorus which commented, repeated, described, and explained, thus bridging the chasm between the writer and his somewhat remote audience.

Shakespeare had to set the bare Elizabethan stage by means of words. As many critics have pointed out, the opening lines of *Hamlet* introduce without any preliminaries the action, the time, the weather, and the mood, creating the entire scene in a few deft words. In *Macbeth*, Shakespeare has a wounded sergeant describe the battle to Duncan, and so inform the audience of the situation before Macbeth actually appears. In *Romeo and Juliet,* Shakespeare made no attempt at realistic settings since the scenes changed so often. Instead, Shakespeare allowed the power of his poetry and the imagination of his audience to build Capulet's house and to transform the bare boards of the stage into a moonlit orchard.

The modern playwright, yielding to economic necessity, writes his work generally for one set or stylizes his play to win greater freedom of movement and perhaps a universality that might be limited by more conventional staging. In *Our Town,* Thornton Wilder returns to the bare stage of Shakespeare but retains the sound effects of radio to lend verisimilitude to the scenes. The theater-in-the-round is another attempt to project the play directly into the audience, in somewhat the same manner as the Elizabethan theater, which thrust a broad peninsula into the sea of groundlings.

The creators of motion pictures have learned to use the panoramic sweep of the camera to stretch over an enormous scene and then to shift quickly to the next point of interest. The camera does not have to linger a moment more than necessary. The audience, therefore, does not have to wait impatiently—as it sometimes does in the theater—for a character to walk down the stairs, if this is only an incidental action. The camera cuts out the extraneous action and places the character in the midst of significance without loss of time or continuity. On the motion picture screen, characterization often becomes a montage of little scenes that are fused by the camera into a single impression. These staccato scenes affect the kind of acting that is required, and therefore most actors prefer the continuity of stage acting to the disjointedness of the motion picture style. The close-up technique of the camera draws the audience right up on the stage and gives the motion picture a focus that the stage play must achieve in other ways. This technique places more emphasis on the cutting and editing, two processes that actually fashion a work of art out of jigsaw pieces.

Television drama is played to an audience of perhaps

three or four people who are seated in the privacy of their living room. The humor that requires the infectious reaction of a "live" audience therefore loses much of its force, and many a television comedian grows old before his years in a frantic effort to remain funny in this most exacting situation. The demands made on an actor differ, too. Mildred Dunnock, at a symposium held at Teachers College, Columbia University, declared:

> On the stage you have the natural sequence of the play to help you. On television . . . you often come to the height of your emotion without anything leading up to it but your imagination or perhaps the narrator's words. I would say that on the stage you also have the feeling of being involved in that special world of the stage . . . the footlights and the barrage of lights—and . . . though you are curiously connected with the audience, you are also curiously detached from the audience.

The television writer, who must conform to the technical laws of his medium, must also often conform to the restrictions imposed by the family audience and by the necessity of attracting advertiser support. The vigor of a theme is often modified to suit a mass audience, and the play itself is written to provide pauses for the insertion of commercials. Yet the prospect of addressing one of the greatest audiences drama has ever known offers a challenging opportunity to the television playwright.

Thus, even a cursory unit on comparative drama will place television in the continuum of the theater. Viewed in this way, *Electra, Macbeth, Our Town, High Noon,* and *Marty* become milestones—though not of equal importance to be sure—on the somewhat devious highway of dramatic literature.

Course in Television

The television unit or a series of television units could be extended to an entire semester's length and thus could be offered as an elective course. The suggestions made below might constitute a reasonable sequence of such units. The teacher will note, however, that each of these units could conveniently be adapted for purposes other than a full course in television. For example, a unit on television criticism, outlined below, could easily serve as a *Brief Unit within the Curriculum* or as an *Extended Unit.* So could a unit on the television industry or the unit which involves a historical analysis of one of television's literary genres (both outlined below). This principle of interchangeable parts will work the other way around as well. That is, the teacher might use all of the categories discussed up to this point as a syllabus for a full course. For example, the teacher, at the very start of his course, might appoint a Television Program Committee, as discussed earlier, whose function it would be to report to the class each Monday on the "pick of the week." Such a committee could make use of *Studies in the Mass Media, TV Guide,* "Look and Listen" in *Scholastic Teacher,* "The Public Arts" in *The English Journal,* monthly program bulletins published by many local stations, Sunday supplements, and other sources of program information. As also discussed earlier, the teacher might appoint a committee which would prepare and maintain attractive bulletin boards about forthcoming programs. Such activities as these, valuable in themselves, could certainly be important features of an entire course on television. Nevertheless, the suggestions made below have not been discussed previously and, in total, represent the body of a complete syllabus.

THE TELEVISION LOG

The teacher might require his students to maintain throughout the semester a television log. This would involve each student in keeping a record of the television programs he viewed in any given week and his evaluation of one or two of them. Such a document not only would be interesting in itself but also could be used by the teacher to evaluate his own and his students' work, especially if each student is persuaded to be entirely honest in his accounting. If the level of a student's criticism remains the same from September to January, the teacher will have good cause to wonder about the value of the course for that student. If the level of criticism rises, the teacher will have cause for rejoicing. Also, by observing the kinds of programs the student has viewed, the teacher will have still another index of success or failure. If at the beginning of the semester, for example, a student indicates that his television viewing is almost exclusively confined to westerns and "cops-and-robbers" shows, the teacher need not be surprised. If at the end of the semester, the student has not diversified his viewing, the teacher needs to re-examine his methods and materials. The teacher, however, should avoid the trap wherein the *number* of hours that the student spends with television is regarded as an index of the student's level of maturation. The number of hours is not nearly so important as the kind of programs viewed and the quality of the student's responses to them.

The television log would naturally be a continuing activity, begun in the first week of the course and maintained throughout the semester. In this sense, it is not properly referred to as a unit. Nevertheless, the teacher might have to spend the entire first week of the course explaining what he means by a television log and perhaps supplying his students with model entries and model evaluations. The evaluations below are examples of the kind of work a teacher might expect from high school students. College students, of course, would produce more sophisticated evaluations.

PROGRAM
Have Gun, Will Travel

DATE
Saturday, June 25, 1960

TIME
9:30—10 P.M.

TYPE
Western

PLOT

The hero of this western, the gunfighter, Paladin, is hired by Jed Gray to teach him how to shoot a gun. Jed tells Paladin that he must learn how to defend himself against a notorious bully in his home town. Paladin feels this is a worthy purpose and proceeds to teach Jed how to be proficient in the art of killing. After the intensive "course" is over, Jed pays Paladin a thousand dollars and returns home. Several weeks later, Jed's father comes to San Francisco (Paladin's home base) and tells Paladin that Jed killed not only the town bully but also several other people, some of whom, for the most part, were minding their own business. Jed apparently has become fascinated by killing. Paladin, feeling responsible for the problem, returns to Jed's home town and tries to convince him to reform. Jed turns on his teacher and challenges him to a draw. Paladin, against his will, accepts the fight and kills Jed. Just before he dies, Jed admits to his father and Paladin that his outlook on life was all wrong.

THEME

The theme would appear to be that people who are proficient in killing other people have a responsibility to be fair, law-abiding, and reasonable. If they are not, other killers, even better than they, will take care of them.

EVALUATION

Although *Have Gun, Will Travel* is generally a fine series, this show was one of Paladin's poorer adventures. For one thing, it was not too believable. When Jed came to Paladin, he had never used a gun in his life. How could he have become such a deadly shot in two or three weeks? For another thing, why did Jed think the only way to handle the bully was to shoot him down? Also, everything in the play was predictable. As soon as Jed asked Paladin to teach him how to shoot, I knew practically the whole story. The show could have been improved if, at the end, Jed killed Paladin, then his father, then the writer of this show.

PROGRAM
The Untouchables

DATE
Thursday, September 8, 1960

TIME
9:30—10:30 P.M.

TYPE
Cops and Robbers

PLOT

The stories in this weekly series are supposed to be based on actual events that took place during the late 1920's and early 1930's. This particular story is about an attempt on the life of Chicago's mayor, Anton Cermak.

Members of Al Capone's "syndicate" decide that Cermak's integrity as a public official is an annoying obstacle to their illegal activities. At first, they hire a lawyer who is instructed to bribe or blackmail Cermak into resigning. Cermak refuses and threatens legal action against the lawyer. The "mob" panics, and to make sure that the lawyer has no chance to name his employers, they have him "taken for a ride." Having failed at nonviolent means of eliminating Cermak, the mob hires two distinguished "torpedoes" to kill him. Fortunately, Eliot Ness and his band of "untouchables" (it seems nobody can bribe them) are alerted to this possibility although they know nothing of the details of the plot. At the last minute, Ness learns these details from a member of the "mob" who is trying to make a deal with the "feds." Thus, Ness and his men foil the plot and at the same time shoot down Cermak's would-be assassins.

THEME

The theme is that crime very often does not pay, especially when dedicated, courageous, and intelligent men are upholding the law. Also, since the big bosses of the "mob" survived this show in order to make trouble in the next show, I guess that another theme is that the fight against crime never ends.

EVALUATION

This show was very gripping, probably because it was acted so well. In the first place, Walter Winchell narrated the program, and his voice and manner gave the impression that we were seeing real history. In the second place, with the exception of Eliot Ness, whose expression and mood never changed, the important characters in the story all seemed very real. They acted the way I imagine people would act under similar circumstances. Even the gangsters were depicted as being frightened or amused or sometimes honest (in their way). In fact, I am beginning to grow rather fond of Frank Nitti (Al Capone's chief helper). In the third place, the program had a great deal of suspense. Since Eliot Ness does not always solve his case and these events were supposed to be true, I really did not know whether Mayor Cermak would be saved. In fact, in the following program he actually was killed, mostly because Ness and his men were not watching the right assassin.

PROGRAM
The Jazz Age (Project 20)

DATE
Friday, August 5, 1960

TIME
10—11 P.M.

TYPE
Documentary

SYNOPSIS

This documentary dealt with the era known as The Jazz Age. The film began with the year 1919 and ended with 1929 at the time of the great stock market crash. Along the way, we were shown some of the important (and unimportant) political, social, economic, literary and athletic events of the times. For example, Charles Lindbergh's nonstop flight from New York to Paris was described in detail, as was his reception upon his return. Babe Ruth was shown hitting a home run in the Yankee Stadium. F. Scott Fitzgerald was shown at work in Paris. People of all kinds were shown in nightclubs and at parties, drinking, dancing, laughing, and generally enjoying themselves. All of this gaiety came to a halt when the stock market crashed.

Fred Allen narrated the program. The music was composed by Robert Russell Bennett.

THEME

The point of this documentary was that between the end of World War I and the beginning of the Depression, many Americans lived gay, thoughtless lives, believing that prosperity and peace would last forever. The music, morals, and customs of the time reflected both the excitement and the immaturity of the age.

EVALUATION

This documentary was the best of all those that *Project 20* has produced. Although some of the film was difficult to see on television, the film researcher, editor, and director did competent jobs in finding, selecting, and arranging pertinent film clips. Even the excerpts from old movies, which were used to show events of which there is no actual photographic record, were convincing. The music conveyed much of the spirit of the times. The tone of the narration was both sarcastic and nostalgic, in the manner of a middle-aged man reviewing the foolish experiences of his youth. Particularly impressive was the negative shot of the stock market, which, at various intervals, was superimposed on the screen to remind the audience that the stock market would soon turn the mood of the Jazz Age inside out.

It is unlikely that elementary school students would be exposed to a full course in television. But for the elementary school teachers who might find the television log useful in some other context, we have reproduced below two examples of television criticism that were actually written by youngsters.

The following evaluations were made by two sixth graders. The evaluations appear exactly as they were written:

Popeye Theater

Time—6:00—7:00

September 28, 1960

I think this is a good show because, they have good entertainment. Especially because comedys are often shown. Also after children finish school for the day they should be able to have time for what they want to do. Also the cartoons are funny to watch. Also in a way the comedys are educational because, what you see the characters doing shows that you shouldn't do these antics, such as poking someone in the eyes. But I think for our grade level that this is a program that isn't to babyish for us.

Popeye Theater

Time—6:00—7:00

September 28, 1960

I watched Popeye Theater without much enthusiasm. Last year Popeye was a favorite and I continually watched it. But soon I saw that the cartoons were the same and no new ideas. I knew the outcome of every cartoon—Popeye eats his spinach and saves Olive Oyl from Bluto.

Popeye Theater has a few good points to but not very many.

ORIGINAL TELEVISION DRAMA

After initiating the television log, the teacher might proceed to a study of original television drama. For this purpose, anthologies of television plays—now being published with increasing frequency—may be used. The following list of plays would be a good representation of television drama at its best: Paddy Chayefsky's *Marty, The Bachelor Party, The Catered Affair;* Rod Serling's *Patterns, Requiem for a Heavyweight;* Tad Mosel's *My Lost Saints;* Reginald Rose's *Twelve Angry Men, Tragedy in a Temporary Town, Thunder on Sycamore Street;* Gore Vidal's *Visit to a Small Planet;* J. P. Miller's *The Rabbit Trap, The Days of Wine and Roses;* Horton Foote's *A Young Lady of Property;* James Costigan's *Little Moon of Alban.*

Most of these plays appear in one anthology or another and thus their scripts may be studied at leisure. At the present moment, technical and legal obstacles prevent the teacher from securing kinescope-recordings or videotapes of these shows, but in the near future, it is possible that some of them will be made available at nominal cost for study in the English classroom. In any case, the teacher would certainly not want to confine this unit to the study of television's past history. He might use for analysis contemporary plays which the students could study as these dramas are presented on the television screen. As suggested previously, the students might discuss, each in its turn, the plot, characterization, theme, sets, and acting in each play. This unit would have essentially two purposes: first, to familiarize the students with the best in television drama, and second, to develop criteria for evaluating television plays. In order to further those aims, the teacher might obtain permission for the students to visit a television studio so that they may better understand the technical problems of producing a play.

At this point, the teacher might proceed to a cross media analysis or any of the following units:

1. A Study of Television Criticism
2. A Study of the Television Industry (including, of course, advertising)
3. Historical Analysis of Westerns (or some other television genre)

A brief outline of each of these units follows.

A STUDY OF TELEVISION CRITICISM

The purpose of this unit is to make students aware of the standards used by professional critics. The students might be required, first, to identify the important television critics; second, to examine their methods of operation; and third, to make judgments about their general competence, their standards, their strong and weak points. Such a unit would possibly involve an analysis of the writings of several of the following critics: Jack Gould, Terrence O'Flaherty, Janet Kern, Frank Judge, Fred Danzig, Marya Mannes, Harry Harris, Bill Ewald, Cynthia Lowry, Robert Lewis Shayon, Gilbert Seldes. The students might construct a kind of boxscore which could be used as a basis of evaluation. An example follows:

PLOT

Has the critic given an accurate summary of the plot?

THEME

Has the critic clarified the meaning of the play?

Has he criticized the author or director for his failure to make it clear?

Has he explained why it is not clear? Or, if it is clear, why?

COMPARISONS AND CONTRASTS

Has the critic compared and contrasted the play with other contemporary productions either by the same author or by other people who have dealt with the same theme?

Has the critic tried to place the work in some larger context?

Has he related it to some aspect of contemporary society?

Has he placed it within some literary tradition?

AUTHOR

Has the critic discussed the author's skill (or lack of it) in writing dialogue? in creating suspense? in evoking a mood?

DIRECTOR

Is the critic aware of the director's contribution to the production? the actors'?

TECHNICAL MATTERS

Has the critic commented on the camera work? the settings? the lighting?

NONLITERARY CRITICISM

When the critic is not dealing with a play, does he discuss a wide range of television's problems? For example, does he inform his readers about the activities of the FCC? about advertising agencies? network policies?

Does he deal with these matters objectively?

Obviously, no one critic will be concerned with all of these things at any one time. Nevertheless, over a period of two or three weeks, the students ought to be able to discern certain patterns in the writing of each critic and perhaps come to some tentative conclusions. The students might discover, for example, that some critics are perceptive reporters and commentators on the legal, economic, and social facts of the television industry but that their methods of judging television drama are poorly defined and inconsistent. The students might also find that some critics are largely interested in gossip. Certainly, we hope they will find some who are adept at analyzing and evaluating television drama. For help in making judgments, the students may be encouraged to cultivate the habit of comparing two or more different reviews of the same programs. In the process they will no doubt discover more about the competence of the critics than of the program. Finally, and inevitably, the students might try their own hand at writing detailed television criticism. The teacher will note that opportunities for the functional use of writing, reading, speaking, and listening will spring up everywhere during this and other units.

A STUDY OF THE TELEVISION INDUSTRY

The purpose of this unit is to provide students with an understanding of the economic and legal contexts within which television operates. As emphasized in Part One of this book, television, like all mass media of communication, is essentially a business, and no adequate comprehension of television's function in society can be achieved unless this relationship is carefully considered.

Perhaps the most productive way to proceed is for the teacher to divide the class into committees, assigning each committee the responsibility to investigate one phase of television and to prepare a series of talks and/or papers on its findings. The following topics might lead to informative studies:

1. The History of Television
2. The Role of the Federal Communications Commission
3. The Impact of Television on Other Media
4. The Role of the Sponsor in Television
5. The Function of Television Networks
6. The BBC Approach
7. Pay Television versus Free Television
8. Educational Television

Each of these topics is obviously too large in scope for even a committee of students to handle, and the teacher will have to help his students refine the project to manageable proportions. He might, for example, prepare an *Inquiry Sheet* for each committee, as follows:

TOPIC
The Role of the Sponsor in Television

REFERENCES
The Age of Television, by Leo Bogart
Broadcasting in America, by Sidney Head
Madison Avenue, USA, by Martin Mayer
Mass Communication, by Erik Barnouw
Mass Communication, by Charles Wright
Television Bureau of Advertising, One Rockefeller Plaza, New York 20, N.Y.

SPECIFIC AREAS TO COVER

1. Find out how much money is spent by American business on television advertising.
2. Define the different methods of advertising on television, e.g. the spot announcement, the participation program.
3. Distinguish the approach to advertising in magazines and newspapers from the approach to advertising on television.
4. List the advantages and disadvantages of our sponsored system of broadcasting.
5. Identify some of the sponsors who combine responsibility to their stockholders with responsibility to artistic integrity.

Providing an Inquiry Sheet for each committee will be no easy task for the teacher. Both Part One of this book and the annotated bibliography will be of service in the teacher's efforts to structure his students' inquiries.

A HISTORICAL ANALYSIS OF THE WESTERN

In Part One of this book, we took pains to point out that much of television's literature derives from older forms of literature. Television's Stuart Bailey, for example, is an extension, even if a blunted one, of Sherlock Holmes or perhaps Poe's M. Dupin. This unit would be a study in depth of one of television's genres (it need not be a western, of course). Its purpose would be to make students aware of literary traditions and in so doing help them relate the present with the past.

If the western is chosen as the form to be studied, it will provide the teacher with a variety of directions in which to go. For example, the teacher might start with the assumption that the western is a modern morality play. The students might then read a medieval morality play—*Everyman* will do well

—and try to find points of similarity between it and a western. A comparison of Everyman himself with, say, Paladin (whose name of course suggests a medieval knight) would be most revealing. Other morality plays might be read, *Mankynd* and *The Castle of Perseverance,* and compared with typical westerns to discover in what ways abstract ideas are made concrete in both forms. In the more competent morality plays such ideas were made interesting and forceful by personification by lively figures confronted with wholly human situations. One suspects that in the more competent westerns (or "cops-and-robbers" stories, for that matter) the same artistry is apparent. (*Wagon Train* and *Naked City* are good examples of this.)

An analysis of the television western suggests still another approach. The teacher might focus the unit on the literature of the frontier. As background, the students might be required to read Francis Parkman's *Oregon Trail* or Henry Nash Smith's *Virgin Land* or Victor Weybright's *Buffalo Bill.* (The teacher might contribute an added dimension of dignity to the unit, if one is needed, by reading to the class Byron's tribute to Daniel Boone in the eighth canto of *Don Juan.*) The students might begin their examination of frontier fiction with James Fenimore Cooper, proceed to the dime novels of the mid-nineteenth century, and then move on to an examination of the westerns and cowboy heroes of Bret Harte, Owen Wister, the movies, and finally, television.

Workshop in Television

At the far end of the spectrum, we come to the workshop in television. A workshop is, of course, possible only where there are technical facilities available either in the school or community. If the workshop is situated near a television studio, the activities can be expanded considerably. Sometimes an arrangement can be made to conduct the workshop in the television studio itself, an enormous advantage for psychological as well as technical reasons. Even if that is not possible, the director of the studio may be induced to permit students to observe a production in preparation and in action, giving the group an appreciation of the role of the producer, the actor, the director, and the cameraman. This appreciation would be enhanced if the professional participants were invited to address the students and discuss the problems and the technique of their craft. In an ideal situation, a far-seeing television station may allow the group to work in conjunction with the staff, helping students in all the activities that are involved in a television production—writing, acting, directing, announcing. A television program, written, produced, and acted by the students themselves and actually televised by the station at a time that would not interfere with commercial commitments, would bring the workshop to an exciting finale; but teachers must realize that many obstacles would probably prevent the dream from becoming a reality. Noncommercial stations, particularly those connected with universities and boards of education, would probably welcome and encourage workshop production. Possibly, even in commercial television, the enthusiasm and the dedication of the students will overcome any initial difficulties.

129

Our purpose in presenting this spectrum of television activities for the English classroom is to encourage teachers to treat the study of television as one aspect of English instruction. We do not suggest for a moment that we have covered every device that can co-ordinate television with classroom work. Teachers all over the country will be able to expand the bands of this spectrum with additional methods they are now using. Nor are we suggesting that teachers start with the simplest of the methods and aspire to the most complex. We cannot expect every high school to develop a television workshop (although it is probably not too much to expect that some high schools and colleges will offer an elective course in television). Circumstances and personal interest will dictate what suggestions each English teacher can or may wish to use. Perhaps in the near future—and feasible procedures are now being investigated—television networks will make television recordings of major productions available for educational use; then teachers can bring actual television programs into the classroom for observation, analysis, and evaluation. The important point to remember is that even the announcement in class of a forthcoming television production will be an acknowledgment that television is an important medium of communication that belongs somewhere in the English curriculum.

Glossary

Some of the terms defined below appear in the text of the book without explanation, for example, *prime time, cutting, picture definition*. Other terms do not appear in the text but are an integral part of the language of television. The terms are arranged into three groups. In Group I are terms used to discuss the production and transmission of television pictures. In Group II are terms used to discuss the television director's art. In Group III are terms used to discuss various aspects of the television industry.

GROUP I

Spectrum: The range of frequencies available to radio and television broadcasting and other services that utilize radio waves is generally referred to as the radio, electromagnetic, or waveband spectrum. Specific sections of the spectrum are reserved for specific uses, such as: maritime and aeronautical radio; long-range radio telegraph and telephone; amateur radio; police, fire department, and forest service communications; radar and telemetric control of missile guidance systems; and AM, FM, and television broadcasting stations.

Channel: A television channel is a segment of the waveband spectrum allocated to each TV station for the transmission of its signals. Each channel is on a specific frequency. The signals of a station must be transmitted on an assigned frequency to avoid interference with other channels.

VHF: The typical TV receiver is equipped to "pick up" signals whose frequencies are between 54 and 216 megacycles per second. This frequency range is called Very High Frequency (VHF) and is segmented into 12 channels (2 through 13).

UHF: The Ultra High Frequency (UHF) range is segmented into 70 channels (14 through 83). The UHF spectrum is almost three times as great as that of VHF. Most television receivers, at present, are not equipped to "pick up" signals in the UHF band.

Live Television: This term is used to describe programs that are performed at the same moment they are telecast to the audience.

131

Picture Definition: This term refers to distinctiveness of detail in the visual image. Since the television picture is actually formed by lines that scan the screen, the greater the number of lines used to compose the picture the better the definition.

Kinescope: A filmed recording of a live production is called a kinescope recording (or simply, a "kine"). Kinescope recordings are made by photographing the program as it is received on the television picture tube.

Video Tape: Video Tape recordings have largely replaced kinescope recordings as a method of preserving television programs for later use. Video taping involves the use of electronic tape instead of motion picture film. The quality of video tape recordings is superior to the quality of kinescope recordings.

GROUP II

Shots: A full view of a scene is referred to as a *long shot;* a nearer view, a *medium shot;* a still nearer view, a *close shot;* and a detailed view, a *close-up*. These terms cannot be meticulously defined. One director's medium shot may differ in closeness from another's. Generally, however, a close-up of a person includes only his head and shoulders. The term *reaction shot* refers to a picture which shows the response of a person to a given situation. During the presidential debates, the question of whether or not reaction shots should be used was much discussed.

Dissolve: Sometimes called a *lap dissolve,* a dissolve describes the process of overlapping the end of one scene on top of the beginning of another. In other words, the first scene fades out as the second scene is fading in.

Cut: A cut is an immediate displacing of one scene with another.

Pan: This term is an abbreviation of *panorama* and refers to a slow, horizontal movement of the camera lens.

Dolly: A dolly is a platform with wheels which facilitites the movement of the camera. The word is used frequently as a verb ("Dolly forward").

GROUP III

Construction Permit: Before a license to operate a new television or radio station is granted, the Federal Communications Commission issues a construction permit to the applicant, setting forth the specifications and conditions that must be met in constructing and equipping the station.

Advertising Agencies: Advertising agencies are intermediaries between the broadcaster and the sponsor. The agency represents the sponsor, often selecting the program the sponsor will finance.

Prime Time: This term refers to choice broadcasting time, which is to say times when the greatest number of viewers are available. 6 P.M. to 11 P.M on weekday nights and 5 P.M. to 11 P.M. on Sundays are generally regarded as prime time.

Ratings: Ratings are estimates of the audience for various programs. There are several organizations which conduct such surveys, for example, American Research Bureau, A. C. Nielsen Co., Trendex, Inc., Pulse, Inc., and the Hooper Index of Broadcast Advertisers.

Pay TV: Pay TV is a television service for which the viewer pays in order to receive a program. The viewer "unscrambles" a distorted picture by inserting a coin or card in a box attached to his television set. Programs are not commercially sponsored since the audience pays for the costs.

NAB Code of Good Television Practice: Approximately 500 television stations subscribe to the NAB Code, a set of minimum standards of good taste. The Code was established by the National Association of Broadcasters.

Selected Bibliography

ACE, Goodman. *The Book of Little Knowledge.* New York: Simon and Schuster, Inc., 1955.

ASHEIM, Lester, ed. *The Future of the Book.* Chicago: University of Chicago Press, 1955.

BACHMAN, John. *The Church in the World of Radio-Television.* New York: Association Press, 1960.

BARNOUW, Erik. *Mass Communication.* New York: Holt, Rinehart, and Winston, Inc., 1956.

BLUM, Daniel. *A Pictorial History of Television.* Philadelphia: Chilton Company—Book Division, 1959.

BOGART, Leo. *The Age of Television.* New York: Frederick Ungar Publishing Co., 1956.

BUSSELL, Jan. *The Art of Television.* London: Faber & Faber, undated.

CHAYEFSKY, Paddy. *Television Plays.* New York: Simon and Schuster, Inc., 1955.

COOPER, Lane, ed. *Plato.* Ithaca, N. Y.: Cornell University Press, 1955.

COWLEY, Malcolm. *The Literary Situation.* New York: The Viking Press, Inc., 1958.

CROSBY, John. *Out of the Blue.* New York: Simon and Schuster, Inc., 1952.

DECKER, Richard. *Plays for Our Time; Motion Pictures, TV, Radio.* New York: Oxford Book Co., Inc., 1959.

EDITORS OF TV GUIDE. *TV Guide Roundup.* New York: Holt, Rinehart, and Winston, Inc., 1960.

EDUCATIONAL POLICIES COMMISSION. *Mass Communication and Education.* Washington: National Education Association, 1958.

ELLIOTT, William, ed. *Television's Impact on American Culture.* East Lansing: Michigan State University Press, 1956.

FISCHER, Edward. *The Screen Arts: A Guide to Film and Television Appreciation.* New York: Sheed & Ward, 1960.

FOOTE, Horton. *Harrison, Texas; Eight Television Plays.* New York: Harcourt, Brace & World, Inc., 1956.

HEAD, Sydney. *Broadcasting in America*. Boston: Houghton Mifflin Co., 1956.

HENRY, Nelson, ed. *Mass Media and Education*. Chicago: The National Society for the Study of Education, 1954.

HIMMELWEIT, Hilde, with A. N. Oppenheim and Pamela Vance. *Television and the Child*. London: Oxford University Press, 1958.

HOGBEN, Lancelot. *From Cave Painting to Comic Strip*. London: Max Parrish, 1949.

INNIS, Harold. *The Bias of Communication*. Toronto: University of Toronto Press, 1951.

JOURNAL OF THE AMERICAN ACADEMY OF ARTS AND SCIENCES. *Mass Culture and Mass Media*. Middletown, Conn.: Wesleyan University Press, 1960.

KAUFMAN, William, ed. *The Best Television Plays, 1950-51*. New York: Merline Press, 1952.

————, ed. *How to Write for Television*. New York: Hastings House, Publishers, Inc., 1955.

————, ed. *Best Television Plays, 1957*. New York: Harcourt, Brace & World, Inc., 1958.

KERR, Walter. "What Good is Television?" *Horizon,* II (March 1960), 4-5, 126-128.

KLAPPER, Joseph. *The Effects of Mass Media*. New York: Bureau of Applied Research, Columbia University, 1949.

————. *Children and Television: A Review of Socially Prevalent Concerns*. New York: Bureau of Applied Social Research, Columbia University, 1954.

————. "What Does Research Show?" *Child Study,* XXXVII (1960), 16-28.

————. *The Effects of Mass Communication*. Chicago: The Free Press of Glencoe, Illinois, 1960.

LARRABEE, Eric. "Our Face to the World." *Horizon,* II (May 1960), 4-9, 122-123.

MANNES, Marya. "Lonely Men and Busy Machines." *The Reporter,* 17 (July 1957), 39-40.

MAYER, Martin. *Madison Avenue, USA*. New York: Harper & Brothers, 1958.

————. "How Good Is TV at Its Best? (Part One)," *Harper's Magazine,* 221 (August 1960), 82-90.

————. "How Good Is TV at Its Best? (Part Two)," *Harper's Magazine,* 221 (September 1960), 85-90.

McLuhan, Marshall. "What the Mass Media Mean to Teachers of English." An address delivered at the 45th Annual Convention of the National Council of Teachers of English, New York, November 24, 1955.

Mosel, Tad. *Other People's Houses—Six Television Plays.* New York: Simon and Schuster, Inc., 1956.

Riesman, David. "Books: Gunpowder of the Mind," *Atlantic Monthly,* 200 (December 1957), 123-130.

Rose, Reginald. *Six Television Plays.* New York: Simon and Schuster, Inc., 1956.

Rosenberg, Bernard, and White, David Manning, eds. *Mass Culture.* Chicago: The Free Press of Glencoe, Illinois, 1957.

Schramm, Wilbur, ed. *The Process and Effects of Mass Communication.* Urbana: Universtiy of Illinois Press, 1954.

————. *Responsibility in Mass Communication.* New York: Harper and Brothers, 1957.

————. "The College Woman and the Mass Media." An address delivered at the Biennial National Convention of the American Association of University Women, June 24, 1959.

————. *Mass Communication,* 2nd ed. Urbana: University of Illinois Press, 1960.

————, ed. *The Impact of Educational Television.* Urbana: University of Illinois Press, 1960.

Seldes, Gilbert. "Radio, TV, and the Common Man," *Saturday Review,* 36 (August 1953), 11.

————. *The Public Arts.* New York: Simon and Schuster, Inc., 1956.

Serling, Rod. *Patterns.* New York: Simon and Schuster, Inc., 1957.

Shayon, Robert Lewis. *Television and Our Children.* New York: Longmans, Green & Co., Inc., 1951.

Siepmann, Charles. *Radio, Television, and Society.* New York: Oxford University Press, 1950.

STEINBECK, John. "How to Tell Good Guys from Bad Guys," in Fiedler, Leslie (ed.). *The Art of the Essay.* New York: Thomas Y. Crowell Company, 1958.

VIDAL, Gore. "The Perils and Rewards of Going into Trade," *The Reporter,* 17 (July 1957), 33-36.

————, ed. *Best Television Plays.* New York: Ballantine Books, Inc., 1956.

WINICK, Charles. *Taste and the Censor in Television.* New York: Fund for the Republic, 1959.

WITTY, Paul. "Television and the High School Student," *Education,* LXXII (1951), 242-251.

————. "Children's Reactions to TV: A Third Report," *Elementary English,* XXIX (1952), 469-473.

————. "School Children and Television." A paper presented at the Annual Meeting of the American Association for the Advancement of Science, Chicago, December 29, 1959.

————. "Televiewing by Children and Youth," *Elementary English,* XXXVIII (1961), 103-113.

WRITERS GUILD OF AMERICA, eds. *The Prize plays of Television and Radio.* New York: Random House, 1956.

WRIGHT, Charles. *Mass Communication: A Sociological Perspective.* New York: Random House, 1959.